Keep
Uncle Sam
From Devouring
Your
Life Savings

By
Stephen M. Rosenberg, C.F.P.

CAREER PRESS
180 Fifth Avenue
P.O. Box 34
Hawthorne, NJ 07507
1-800-CAREER-1
201-427-0229 (outside U.S.)
FAX: 201-427-2037

KEEP UNCLE SAM FROM DEVOURING YOUR LIFE SAVINGS
ISBN 1-56414-120-9, $14.95
Cover design by Dean Johnson Design, Inc.
Printed in the U.S.A. by Book-mart Press

To order this title by mail, please include price as noted above, $2.50
handling per order, and $1.00 for each book ordered. Send to: Career Press,
Inc., 180 Fifth Ave., P.O. Box 34, Hawthorne, NJ 07507.
Or call toll-free 1-800-CAREER-1 (Canada: 201-427-0229) to order using
VISA or MasterCard, or for further information on books from Career Press.

Legal Disclaimer: This book is neither an attempt to provide legal advice
nor a substitute for the same. It is intended to provide accurate and
authoritative information regarding the subject matter covered. It is
provided with the understanding that the publisher is not engaged in
rendering legal, accounting, or other professional service. If legal advice or
other expert assistance is required, the services of a competent professional
should be sought.

Library of Congress Cataloging-in-Publication Data

Rosenberg, Stephen M., 1944-
    Keep Uncle Sam from devouring your life savings / by Stephen M.
    Rosenberg.
        p.   cm.
    Includes index.
    ISBN 1-56414-120-9 : $14.95
    1. Estate planning--United States--Popular works. I. Title.
KF750.Z9R673   1994
346.7305'2--dc20
[347.30652]
                                                                 93-45847
                                                                     CIP

Dedication

*This book is dedicated to my wife, Nancy, for her continuous
love and support, and to my children, David and Jeffrey,
who are an important part of my life.*

Thanks

The author thanks the following attorneys (in alphabetical order)
for their assistance and counsel in reviewing this book.

Steven R. Bone, J.D., CLU, is the director of Legal Support
Services for an Indianapolis, Indiana firm that specializes in the
implementation and third-party of administration of charitable remainder trusts.

Kelly R. Burke, J.D., is an attorney who devotes a substantial portion of his practice to estate planning and asset protection. He is a
member of the Estate, Probate and Tax Section of the Georgia State
Bar and makes himself available as a spokesperson on matters of
estate planning.

Gregory Diefenderfer, J.D., CFP, is a former bank trust department officer and legal consultant for a major life insurance company.

In addition, I would like to thank Ann Peterson, a vice-president
with my firm, who took precious time from working with her clients to
make a tremendous contribution with ideas and thoughts. I couldn't
have done it without her.

Contents

Part IV - Protection During Your Lifetime

Part V - Special Planning Situations

Preface

I consider myself very fortunate to be working in a field where I can help people accomplish their financial goals. Other than saving people's lives or improving their health, I can think of no profession more satisfying.

Helping people control their estates using the easiest and least costly methods provides a tremendous service to the public. As a result of efforts by myself and others in my field, Americans can leave more to their families by reducing the amount that is confiscated by Uncle Sam. They can take care of their loved ones upon their death or disability. They can provide for their minor children, adult children and grandchildren in the manner they choose. They can meet their charitable goals using methods that are advantageous to themselves and their favorite charities. And they can accomplish all this, and more, at minimum cost.

That's what they *can* do. Unfortunately, most *don't*. It's no secret that most people do no planning at all. So the obvious questions are: Why do people *knowingly leave* their children's fate in the hands of the probate court? Why do they *pay more* estate taxes than necessary? Why do they *incorrectly structure* their life insurance? Why do they put themselves in a *difficult position* in the event of their disability or mental incapacity? Why do they *tie up their estates* for years in the court system? Why do they *pay unnecessary* capital gains tax on the sale of assets? Why do they *subject their families* to needless publicity? Why do they choose not to solve those problems?

I believe one reason this occurs is because of a general lack of useful estate planning information. Sure, there are magazine articles here and there. There are a slew of books on living trusts. But there has been no single source devoted to explaining the various ideas in simple, everyday language that you can understand.

People make decisions based on suggestions from friends and neighbors, and bits of information they pick up in the paper. To make it even worse, there are many well-intentioned "professionals" who make recommendations to clients based on information that is outdated, incomplete or just plain wrong. So you and your family suffer.

The best way to counter bad advice is through education. Since I am not an attorney, I have deliberately avoided legal-ese and confusing terminology in this book. To the contrary, I have set forth, in simple, easy-to-understand language, various estate planning methods. I have put before you most of the estate planning problems you will face, and some thoughts toward working to solve them. But, and this is very important, the purpose of this book is not to give legal advice by providing counsel and "do-it-yourself" forms. It is not aimed at teaching shortcuts to avoid "The System" and save legal fees.

Rather, its purpose is to provide, in an easy-to-understand format, valuable information to help you in your long-range planning. Unlike many people who author financial books, I am not an advocate of do-it-yourself planning. I believe that good legal work by a competent attorney is vital to your financial security. Estate planning is different from fixing a leaky faucet or wallpapering your home. This is serious stuff that you must leave up to professionals. Do-it-yourself estate planning is like trying to slay a dragon—you'll probably end up getting burned.

This book will prepare you to move forward toward meaningful planning. It will help you get your thoughts together. By reading this book and following through, you will accomplish your goals and avoid doing to yourself and your family what most Americans do.

One final point. The largest obstacle we face in estate planning is that we don't think we have a problem until we have a problem. While that might sound confusing, it's not meant to be. The fact is, it doesn't matter how your property is owned until you need to sell it. It doesn't matter who you name as guardian of your children as long as you or your spouse are alive. It doesn't matter who your insurance company is until you have a claim. It doesn't matter what your estate tax liability is until you die. In sum, until you become disabled or die, you have no problems. But once that occurs, the problems present themselves. By then, it's usually too late.

Rather than waiting for disaster to strike, we are going to look at these problems in advance. We are going to investigate planning methods and explore how to use them to save you and your family time, aggravation and expense. Please join me as we travel through the maze of estate planning. It is with confidence that I say it will be one of the most profitable journeys of your entire life.

Introduction

What is Washington Going to Do to You Next?

The Omnibus Budget Reconciliation Act of 1993 (OBRA) was only the latest step by Washington to increase your tax burden. Although its impact on smaller estates was minimal, I believe there are dark clouds on the horizon.

In 1992, there was an attempt in Congress to reduce the exemption to $200,000. Through the efforts of a number of us, that attack was repelled. However, don't let your guard down. I predict that within the next two years, some form of legislation will pass in Washington that will be devastating to your estate. This will take one or more of several forms: a reduction in your estate tax exemption, probably to $200,000; elimination of your unlimited marital deduction; a cap on the number of gifts you can make each year; an elimination of the "step-up" in basis at death; or a general increase in rates.

As of this writing, it is impossible to know what Congress is going to do. Of course, that is always the case. However, in Chapter 22, I explain how the most likely change, the reduction in the exemption from the current level of $600,000 will affect you. It is vital that you stay abreast of the news from Washington. It can only get worse.

Part I

Traditional
Planning

One

What is Estate Planning, and Why is It Important?

One of my professors once told me that when discussing a complex subject, start from the beginning so everybody knows specifically what you're talking about. Define the terms you are using so there can be no doubt.

So let's start by defining estate planning. You've heard it used by many people, but the definition always seems to vary depending upon the intentions of the speaker. If we are going to accomplish our goals in this book, we must start from common ground.

Definition

Let me give you the definition of estate planning that I developed for my use in working with clients. In my opinion, it expresses exactly what ideal estate planning should accomplish.

Estate planning is the process by which, during your life and after your death, you control your property in the manner you desire, minimizing all fees, taxes and court interference, preserving for yourself, your family, and those you choose, the estate you have worked so hard to create.

That is a long definition that says it all. But this is your book, and any planning should meet your goals. So let's take that definition and restate it as a goal:

*"During **my** life and after **my** death, I want to control and distribute **my** property in the manner I desire, minimizing all fees,*

12

> *taxes and court interference, preserving for **myself, my** family, and those **I** choose, the estate **I** have worked so hard to create."*

Read that definition again. Notice the emphasis. It is on "me" and "my," unlike so much planning that seems to have no direction. My definition gives you the opportunity to take care of *your* concerns, not anybody else's. If this sounds a bit selfish, so be it. You deserve to be the master of your own estate.

Read the definition again. Notice it doesn't just say "I want to pass my estate to my family." Estate planning is much more involved than that. With proper estate planning, you take care of yourself and your family *while you are alive, as well as after your death.* Isn't that what you really want? Don't you want to take care of yourself while you are alive? Don't you want to control the distribution of your assets after your death? Don't you want to eliminate expenses and taxes? And don't you want to stay out of court? Don't you really want to keep the vultures away? Yet, I would bet that if I reviewed your current estate plan, it wouldn't satisfy any of the conditions of my definition, let alone the entire definition.

Let's make it "our" definition

During the course of the book, we are going to cover important estate planning ideas. I will refer often to those ideas as they relate to my definition of estate planning. At this point, I am going to make the assumption that my definition makes sense to you. Therefore, from now on, I will call this "our" definition of estate planning.

Simplistic approach

Many people tell you that the purpose of estate planning is to pass your estate in an organized manner to your heirs upon your death. I think that is much too simplistic. While utilizing proper strategies at your death is important, there are many problems that you face during your *lifetime* that you can only solve with proper estate planning. Additionally, there are steps you can take to reduce the cost, pain and uncertainty of the entire process.

Nevertheless, in spite of the more sophisticated methods available, the average person with whom I consult has a simple will and not much more. They have never considered problems that might occur before death. They have never thought about the consequences after death. They haven't considered the problems their surviving spouse and children will face. They just have a simple will. Period. Nothing more, nothing less. Unfortunately, this type of plan doesn't protect you against all the vultures waiting to devour or play havoc with your estate.

Wait a minute! Haven't we been taught all our lives that as long as we have a will everything will be OK? Haven't we been told that the only reason most people run into problems is that they don't have a will?

Yes, that is exactly what we've been taught. But in my opinion, wills alone are not the answer. *Simple wills are a simplistic attempt to solve a complex problem.* Estate planning is a complex issue requiring complex solutions.

Poor planning

Having spent many years in the financial industry, I have seen the results of inadequate planning. The devastation wrought on families is shocking. It is sad to see widows and children left in the lurch, not necessarily by *lack* of planning, but because of *improper* planning. You see, the desire was there, but the strategy was faulty.

Problems you can face

Let me share with you a few of the dragons that can devour your estate.

- A disability keeps you from handling your finances.
- A surviving spouse is unable to handle money.
- Minor children inherit money.
- An heir contests your will.
- Relatives fight over custody of your children.
- Attorneys' fees eat up the estate.
- Time delays slow down the transfer of your assets.
- Adult children fritter away their inheritance.
- Disabled children need continual care.
- Estate taxes gobble up to 55 percent of your estate.

- Probate judges make rulings affecting your children.
- A nursing home stay consumes your assets.
- Business interests can't be sold.
- Lawsuits need to be settled.
- Property is titled incorrectly.
- Fire sales are required to pay estate taxes.

This list could go on for pages and pages. These are just a few of the problems I will address. What it all means is that the dragons are out there looking for the opportunity to take pieces of your estate. In my experience, traditional planning doesn't address these problems. In fact, usually, it only serves to create them.

Conclusion

If we are going to keep the dragons away from your estate, we must work toward creating the proper estate plan that will achieve your financial goals.

Proper estate planning can provide tremendous benefits to you and your loved ones. You can rest easy, knowing that you have taken care of your family. And as a bonus, you will save yourself and your family thousands, and in some cases millions, of your hard-earned dollars.

Nothing is more rewarding to me than helping a client resolve his or her potential problems. When it's over, everybody feels good. I'll never forget one situation in particular when a client grabbed my hand and said, "Now I can sleep at night knowing my children will be taken care of." Isn't that what it is all about? Isn't proper estate planning an extension of your concern for your family?

As you continue through this book, I hope that you will remember this story and relate to that person's feelings. Nothing can replace the emotional warmth you feel when you have done something good for others, especially when the *others* are those you love and care about.

Two

What Are the Ways of Holding Title?

As I stated previously, proper planning requires addressing a multitude of issues and answering many questions. It also involves gathering data concerning your present financial situation. And in that process, the question of ownership arises. How is your home titled? In whose names are your bank accounts? Who owns your stocks and bonds? How are your brokerage accounts titled?

If you're like most people, you've given little or no thought about how you titled their assets. It was probably done as a matter of convenience. Nevertheless, the consequences of your actions can be enormous, and can leave the door open for the dragons.

Holding title to property, such as real estate, securities, bank accounts, automobiles, etc., seems so simple that we hardly give it a second thought.

> **Attorney:** "How do you want your new home titled?"
> **Client:** "In both of our names."
> **Attorney:** "No problem."

It is so simple, it's scary. Unfortunately, it's *too* simple. When decisions as important as this are made without sufficient thought, they can result in mistakes. Let's review the various ways to hold property, along with the workings and ramifications of each.

1. Sole ownership

How titled. As a sole owner, you hold the title in your name:

"William S. York."

Control during life. Since you are the only owner of the property, you maintain 100-percent control over it. You can do whatever you want with that property: sell it, use it as collateral or give it away. You, and you alone, have complete control.

Disposition upon death. As sole owner of this property, you can pass it in any manner you want. While many other forms have built-in procedures upon death, this passes one of two ways: according to your will or according to the rules of your state (if you don't have a will).

Advantages. Sole ownership has the following advantages.

- It is simple to establish; it doesn't require anybody's signature but your own.
- It is easy to control; you don't have to worry about the approval of other parties.
- The property receives a "stepped-up" basis upon your death. This subject is discussed in Chapter 15.
- It passes according to the terms in your will.

Disadvantages. Sole ownership also has disadvantages.

- Since you alone control the property, transfers during a period of disability are difficult, and often require living probate.
- The property must go through probate upon your death.
- You must arrange for the property to pass upon death.
- The entire value is included in your estate upon death.
- There are higher settlement expenses upon death than other methods of ownership.

2. Tenancy in common

How titled. As tenants in common, you own the property with another person or persons:

"William S. York and Allen M. Hutchins."

Control during life. If there are two owners, you each own half. Many people call this an undivided interest. Although there may be several owners, you alone have control over your own portion. You can sell or pledge your portion, but you don't have control over the entire property. Total control is possible only when all parties agree.

Disposition upon death. Upon your death, you can leave your portion to whomever you want in your will, if you have one. Otherwise, it will pass according to the laws of your state.

Advantages. Tenants in common has several advantages.

- You have complete control over your interest.
- It is an effective technique for income splitting.
- It passes according to your instructions in your will.
- It receives a "stepped-up" basis on the decedent's share (see Chapter 15).

Disadvantages. Tenants in common also has its disadvantages.

- It can get cumbersome if there are many tenants.
- Transfer of your share is difficult if you become disabled.
- Your share of the property must go through probate upon your death.
- You have control over only your interest; you have no voice in what your co-tenants do.
- You can easily end up with an incompatible co-owner upon either the death of the present co-owner or upon the sale of his or her share.
- It is subject to administrative expenses upon your death.

3. Joint tenants with rights of survivorship

How titled. With joint tenants with rights of survivorship, you own the property with another person or persons:

"William S. and Patricia F. York, JTWROS."

Control during life. Each of the joint tenants owns 100 percent of the asset. Yet neither tenant alone has control. Make sense? I hope not, because it shouldn't. It's one of many contradictions in the law—some call it a "legal fiction." It is a difficult issue when dealing with control. If you want to sell your share, while it is cumbersome and difficult, it is possible with court intervention. As a rule, it is easiest to sell when all parties sign. But as an individual tenant, you are limited by realities. While you probably can sell your portion, the person buying it may never realize anything, because the last survivor gets it.

Disposition upon death. The factor that separates this type of property from all other types is what happens upon death. When this type of property is properly titled, which means including the phrase (or similar phrase) "Joint Tenants With Rights of Survivorship," the last surviving tenant gets the property. If you, your husband and your brother own an office building as joint tenants, and you and your husband die, then your brother automatically ends up with the property. It is a classic case of whoever lives the longest wins.

Advantages. The advantages of joint tenancy are as follows.

- It is easy to establish; no special paperwork is required.
- Joint tenancy is inexpensive to set up.
- Property avoids probate until the death of the last tenant.
- The property automatically goes to the surviving tenant(s).
- There are no administrative expenses at death of the first tenant.

Disadvantages. The disadvantages of joint tenancy are discussed in the following chapter.

4. Tenants by the entirety

How titled. Tenants by the entirety is used in a few states and is only for titling property between husband and wife.

"William and Patricia York, Tenants by the Entirety."

Control during life. Neither tenant alone has any control during his or her life. This type of ownership can only be severed with the consent of both parties.

Disposition upon death. Like joint tenants, this form of ownership allows for the survivorship feature that automatically passes the property to the surviving spouse.

Advantages. Tenants by the entirety has several advantages.

- It is easy to establish.
- The property automatically passes to the surviving spouse upon death.
- It avoids probate at first death.

Disadvantages. There are also several disadvantages.

- You have no control over the property without the approval of your spouse.
- The property goes through probate upon the death of the second spouse.
- You have no control over the disposition of the property at your death; it automatically goes to the survivor.
- Only half the property receives a "stepped-up" basis at the first death.
- This ownership form provides no planning flexibility.

5. Life estate

How titled. The life estate is unique to certain states. With this form of ownership, one person leaves another person, usually a spouse, the right to live in and enjoy certain property, after which it goes to a named party, usually children.

Control during life. The party with the life estate has no control over the property during his or her life, only the right to use it.

Disposition upon death. The property automatically passes to the beneficiaries of the life estate.

Advantages. There are only two advantages to a life estate.

- It provides the life tenant with a place in which to live.
- It avoids probate at death.

Disadvantages. There are several significant disadvantages.

- The life tenant must be prudent in the care of property to remain in it.
- The life tenant is at the mercy of the heirs.

- The life tenant is responsible for any expense in maintaining the property.
- The life tenant cannot borrow against the property for maintenance, or any other emergency.
- For these reasons, most attorneys avoid life estates and instead recommend some form of trust to provide more flexibility.

6. Irrevocable living trust

How titled. An irrevocable living trust is a special form of ownership in which the property is titled in the name of a trust:

"Robert Hayes, trustee, or his successor in trust, under the William S. York Irrevocable Trust, dated October 13, 1993."

Control during life. The property in the trust is under the control of the trustee, who cannot be the grantor (trustmaker). Unlike the revocable living trust, where you can be the trustee of your own trust and have complete control, an irrevocable trust is just the opposite. While you can name the trustees initially, you have no control at all over your property. As the name implies, the trust cannot be revoked.

Disposition upon death. The property in the trust will pass according to the instructions contained in the trust document.

Advantages. The irrevocable trust has several advantages.

- It reduces the size of the estate (and thus the taxes) of the trustmaker by removing the property from his or her estate.
- It further reduces those potential taxes by removing the growth on those assets from the estate.
- The trust can be drawn to provide income for the trustmaker.
- Depending upon state law, the property is protected from creditors of the grantor.
- Depending on its provisions, it could be used to protect assets in the case of a nursing home stay. (See Chapters 24 and 25.)
- An irrevocable trust can be used to hold assets for minors.

Disadvantages. The irrevocable trust has several disadvantages.

- Once the trust has been established and funded, you have no control at all over any aspect of the property in the trust.
- In case of emergency, the trust cannot be revoked.
- Because you are irrevocably transferring the property, it is subject to gift tax implications.

7. Revocable trust

This unique form of ownership is discussed in detail in Chapters 7, 8, 12, 13 and 14.

8. Community property

Not to pick on my friends out west, but there are always some people who like to gum up the works. That is what we face in community property states. There are a handful of states that have a different set of rules when it comes to property. Therefore, such issues as property ownership, trusts, gifts, life insurance and gifts to minors need to be addressed for those folks. Although all these states are considered community property states, each has its own particular rules. Check with your estate planning attorney and other professionals to learn how your respective state's rules apply to you.

The community property states. The following states have special rules that dictate the ownership rights of property between husband and wife:

Arizona	New Mexico
California	Texas
Idaho	Washington
Louisiana	Wisconsin
Nevada	

The rules of ownership. The basis of ownership in these states is determined by when the property was acquired. Whereas in most states, property can belong to one or the other spouse, it is a bit different here. Two kinds of property are involved.

Separate property is that property that was acquired before marriage. As long as it remains titled in one spouse's name, it retains separate property status. Additionally, if one spouse inherits property or receives it as a result of a gift, it is separate property belonging to that one spouse.

Community property is that property that was found after marriage. In this case, each spouse owns a 50-percent undivided interest in the property. It doesn't matter who earned the money. It doesn't matter which spouse made the purchase. It belongs equally to each spouse. In addition, if separate property is sold and the proceeds are added to community property, then it takes on the characteristics of community property and is owned 50-50 by each spouse. If the title of separate property is eventually titled in the name of both spouses, it becomes community property.

Passing property at death. Unlike joint tenancy property that automatically passes to the other spouse, community property operates like tenants in common. Each party can pass his or her interest as he or she wants. As a result, community property passes according to the deceased spouse's will. If you haven't taken steps to express your wishes in a will (or a trust), the property will pass according to the intestate laws of your state. Since the surviving spouse already owns half the property, the deceased spouse has the right to leave his or her half to anyone he or she chooses. But if the spouse wants it to go to the surviving spouse, it is imperative that he or she has a will (or trust) stating those intentions.

Gifting. While a spouse in a noncommunity property state can make a separate gift out of his or her own property, in community property states gifts made from community property are considered joint gifts. In fact, some states prohibit one spouse from making a gift from community property without the consent of the other spouse. One major difference between community and noncommunity states comes in the paperwork for joint or "split" gifts. In noncommunity property states, a split gift of $20,000 from both spouses requires a federal gift tax return, although no tax is due. However, in community property states, such a gift is considered a $10,000 gift from each spouse. Therefore, no gift tax return need be filed. If a gift exceeds the $10,000 exclusion, their lifetime exemption will be reduced by one-half of the gift over the $10,000 exemption. (Gifting is covered in Chapter 15.)

Revocable living trusts. Whereas in noncommunity property states separate trusts can be used for married couples, in community property states joint trusts are almost always used. Remember, the community property belongs to both spouses. You cannot split the property and put it in separate trusts. As a result, a joint trust is used with both husband and wife as trustmakers. Additionally, the trust will include language to the effect that upon divorce or revocation of the trust (and each spouse should have the right to revoke), the property will come out of the trust as it went in, thus protecting the interests of each spouse.

Conclusion

Review your property and make sure that the form of title coincides with your goals. Think about why the property is titled the way it is, and ask yourself if that is what you really want. As you can see, the ramifications are many.

Three

What Are the Problems With Joint Tenancy?

To the average couple, joint tenancy is the best way to hold property. Its popularity is due to the fact that it is easy and inexpensive. However, knowledgeable planners know there are dragons waiting to pounce.

JTWROS (Joint Tenants With Rights Of Survivorship) is so simple because it sounds so good—"I love you, honey, and I want you to own this stock when I die." But it can also create some problems. It has been called "the poor man's estate plan" because it costs nothing to establish and avoids probate and attorneys. Unfortunately, in their desire to save attorneys' fees, many people take the wrong steps and create additional problems.

Let's go back to our definition of estate planning.

"During my life and after my death, I want to control and distribute my property in the manner I desire, minimizing all fees, taxes and court interference, preserving for myself, my family, and those I choose, the estate I have worked so hard to create."

Does joint tenancy fulfill this definition? It might save attorney fees and avoid court interference since it bypasses probate (at least at the first death). But do you really have control over your property during your life and after your death? You may answer "yes." I disagree.

Problems with joint ownership

No control over property at death. One of the major disadvantages with joint ownership is one that most people never consider: You

25

have no control over the ultimate disposition of the property. Sure, you can assume the other joint tenant will receive it. But what you cannot be certain of is who will ultimately end up with it.

> *Bob Miller and JoAnn Sullivan, brother and sister, owned a condo on the Gulf that both families shared. For convenience, they titled it "Bob Miller and JoAnn Sullivan, JTWROS." Two years after they purchased it, Bob died. Who received Bob's half? His wife? No. His kids? No. His sister, JoAnn, became sole owner. Remember, it passed to the surviving tenant.*

*   *   *

> *Three businessmen owned a building together. They titled it "Bob Miller, and Bert Levine, and Ted Lee, Joint Tenants." Who owned that property? Remember in the last chapter I said that they each owned 100 percent of it! What happened when Bob died? Did his wife then own his share? No! Bert and Ted then owned the entire building. If Bert dies, Ted will own the whole thing. What a deal! What a disaster!*

No control over property while you are alive. Another problem with joint tenancy is you have no control while you are alive. Because there are at least two tenants, all must sign before doing anything. This can be a blessing or a problem. If the joint owners don't trust each other, then it is helpful to require both signatures. However, if only spouses are involved, there hopefully is a trusting relationship.

Since every transaction requires all tenants to sign, what happens if one is unable to sign because of a physical or mental disability? The other must go through a process known as "living probate," which is discussed in detail in Chapter 23.

> *Bob and Mary Bork owned their home together. Bob was in an accident and ended up in a coma. Mary wanted to sell the house. Enter the dragon. Both names were on the deed, and Bob couldn't sign. Mary visited her attorney. He informed Mary that she should apply for guardianship of Bob (called the conservator in some states). This caused her to go through a process that was not only embarrassing, but expensive as well.*

*   *   *

> *Julio and Maria Gonzales had a brokerage account as joint tenants. While Mr. Gonzales was out of the country attending a convention, Maria needed some money. She called her broker and*

requested a check from their joint money market account. It arrived in the mail, payable to "Julio Gonzales and Maria Gonzales, JTWROS." Maria went to the bank and explained to the teller that her husband was out of the country. The teller politely informed her that she could not cash the check unless it was endorsed by both parties.

Now, I am not so naive as to think that spouses don't sign each other's names on checks. Nevertheless, it's not legal. A bank won't cash a check if it is aware of the forgery.

Much of this is probably news to you. Joint tenancy is so common that most people don't think that there can be any problems. But as you will see throughout the book, if you are going to plan properly, you must identify potential problems in advance, and then take the necessary steps to avoid them.

Doesn't avoid probate—only postpones it. One of the main reasons clients tell me they hold property as joint tenants is that they want to avoid probate. Again, this sounds good. But is it accurate? Does joint tenancy property really avoid probate? Yes and no. While it does avoid probate at the death of the first tenant, the property will have to go through probate at the final death. So you have not avoided probate, you have just postponed it.

Jane and Ralph McCall owned their home and a brokerage account as joint tenants. They had four children. Jane was killed in an accident. The property automatically passed to Ralph at Jane's death. At that point the property was in Ralph's name alone. Upon his death, it will pass according to his will. Whether he dies with or without a will doesn't matter. The property must still go through probate.

You can see that although joint property avoids probate, it only does so when at least one joint tenant survives. At some point, the last tenant is going to die, and the property will go through probate. Joint tenancy, therefore, only postpones the inevitable.

Property can pass to unintended heirs. An additional problem with joint tenancy is your heirs may not end up with your property.

Bob and Susan Miller owned their home as joint tenants. Bob died, and Susan became sole owner. Two years later she remarried.

After a few more years, her new husband suggested that she put the house in both their names. After all, "You do love me, don't you, honey?" "Of course, I do." At that point, the owners of the house were Stan and Susan Johnson, JTWROS. Then Susan died. Who owned the house? Bob's kids? Not on your life! Stan owned it, and Bob and Susan's kids were left out. I don't think that is what Bob would have wanted.

Results in problems upon disability. One of the problems often overlooked is what will happen upon mental incapacity of one of the tenants. What happens if you own your home jointly with your spouse and he or she becomes mentally incapacitated? This is a subject in itself and will be covered in detail in Chapter 23.

Can result in estate taxes for party not receiving property. This can be one of the cruelest problems of all. Let's review our first case:

Bob Miller and JoAnn Sullivan, brother and sister, owned a condo on the Gulf that both families shared. For convenience, they titled it "Bob Miller and JoAnn Sullivan, JTWROS." Two years after they purchased it, Bob died. As a result, JoAnn ended up with all the property. In addition to the fact that Bob's family did not receive his share of the condo, there was another problem: His half of the condo was included in his estate for estate tax purposes. Talk about a kick in the head!

Creates havoc with estate tax planning. I don't want to get too far ahead of myself, since estate taxes will be discussed shortly. Nevertheless, this is one of the biggest estate planning blunders I see.

Rick and Ann Dent's attorney told them they had an estate tax problem that had to be addressed. To reduce their potential taxes, he drew up a trust within their will. (Testamentary trusts are discussed in Chapter 12.) However, they continued to own their property jointly. When Rick died, none of his property made it into the trust, because jointly owned property automatically passes to the surviving spouse—in this case Ann. This error cost them hundreds of thousands of dollars in estate taxes.

Property at risk in the event of lawsuit against either party. We live in a lawsuit-happy society. People are suing each other for practically no reason at all. This means that you must consider how you are going to protect your assets. While this is discussed in detail in Chapter 27, it is worth noting here that joint tenancy is the worst way to protect your property from a lawsuit.

> *John Robinson was in the real estate business. He owned a number of rental properties throughout town. All the properties were titled in his name alone. However, his home and his stock portfolio were jointly held with his wife, Janie. One night, a fire consumed one of his rental properties. Several people were killed and injured. He was hit with a rash of lawsuits by the tenants and families of the deceased. While he had liability insurance, it wasn't sufficient to cover the losses. Therefore, all his other property was attached, including the property held jointly with his wife. They lost everything!*

Joint tenancy with a child

When I discuss estate planning with clients, there are always those who say, "I've got everything taken care of. When my husband dies, I'll just put this property in joint tenancy with my daughter Jill. Then when I die, she will automatically receive it free from probate."

Sounds great. Of course, this assumes that you and your husband won't die together. But I'll give you the benefit of the doubt and follow through with your scenario.

> *Ralph and Carol McNeil maintained several brokerage accounts as joint tenants. Ralph died and left the accounts to Carol, free from probate. Carol wanted to make sure the accounts would avoid probate at her death and changed the title to "Carol McNeil and Jill Baker (her daughter), JTWROS."*

Are there potential problems here? I can think of a few.

Creates a potential gift. By titling the accounts in joint tenancy with Jill, Carol made a gift to Jill. Now I don't want to get ahead of myself, because gifting is discussed in Chapter 15. But when you put property into joint ownership with someone other than your spouse, there are potential gift tax problems. According to the IRS, Carol made a gift of 50 percent of the value to Jill when she put her name on the title, assuming it was a completed gift at the time.

Opens property to lawsuit against either party. This was covered earlier in this chapter. What if Jill gets sued? OK, Jill is a model citizen. She is so perfect, she didn't even need braces. But something bad could happen. Let's imagine the following scenario.

One rainy day Jill is driving down the street, hits a deep puddle, and her car spins into the path of a school bus full of cute elementary kids. The bus comes to a sudden halt in a ditch and a dozen kids are hospitalized. About a month later, the lawsuits come rolling in. Poor Jill, model citizen, perfect wife and mother, is the defendant in a dozen lawsuits. Now her assets are at risk, and guess what are some of her assets? That's right! The brokerage accounts on which she is a joint tenant with her mother are included. And not just 50 percent of the value is at risk, but all of it. Carol risked losing all of her money by putting it in a joint account with Jill.

Property at risk in divorce. What happens to the money if Jill gets divorced? Her husband can claim (and probably rightly so) that the money is part of the marital estate.

Passing property to siblings. Let's assume none of that happens. Everything goes according to plans. Carol holds the property jointly with Jill, and then Carol dies. Again, it's imagination time.

Upon Carol's death, Jill receives the money. She remembers her mother's wishes: "Share my assets with your brothers." Now Jill could be mean and say to her brothers, "Where were you when Mom needed help? Where were you when Mom had to be driven to the doctor? Where were you when I had to pay for a nurse? I deserve all the money." Jill could do that because the money is all hers. Carol left it to her as the surviving tenant. (Since a will doesn't control joint tenancy property, it doesn't matter what instructions the will contains.)

But wait, Jill is the model daughter, so she gives her brothers their shares. Another dragon. Know what it is? Since the money belongs to Jill, she makes a gift when she gives her brothers their shares.

Can inadvertently disinherit your children. Many people try to avoid Carol's problem by titling their property in the names of all their children. Let's look what might happen.

Carol decides to title her property in the names of herself and her children: Jill, Robert and Ronald. However, Ronald dies first. Therefore, when Carol dies, the property is left to Jill and Robert. What about Ronald's children? They're out of luck. Of course, Jill and Robert could decide to give them some money, but then they'd be making a gift, as we will see later!

Conclusion

The fact is that joint tenancy, that bastion of American estate planning, is a disaster waiting to happen. This is one of those areas of estate planning in which people blindly act without considering the consequences, because they don't realize that there might be unfavorable repercussions. But there can be, and you should be aware of them.

And, there is another potential disaster: minor children ending up with the property. That subject is covered in Chapter 10.

Let's go back to our definition now.

"During my life and after my death, I want to control and distribute my property in the manner I desire, minimizing all fees, taxes and court interference, preserving for myself, my family, and those I choose, the estate I have worked so hard to create."

Is there much about joint tenancy that meets this definition? Because of all the potential problems, I don't think so.

Four

What Are the Advantages and Disadvantages of Wills?

As far back as I can remember, attorneys and estate planners have preached the importance of wills. Publication after publication has exhorted the general public to make a will. They have told us the problems of dying without one and suggested that prudent planning requires a will.

That theory was shattered in 1965 when Norman Dacey wrote the best seller, *How to Avoid Probate*. His book started a revolution away from probate that, if anything, is even stronger today.

Dying without a will

As often as we've been told that wills are necessary, only 30 percent of the population has one. The vast majority die "intestate," which means without a will. But not to worry. Even if you die intestate, you do technically have a will:

"I, being of questionable mind, hereby instruct the legislature of my state, in its infinite wisdom, to determine where my assets should go upon my death. Further, they can decide who cares for my children and how their money should be spent. I fully understand that this will occur because I have chosen not to make those decisions myself."

As you can see, if you don't have a will, your property passes according to the laws of your state. I'm sure it's a comforting thought to know that your state legislature has a plan for the distribution of your assets.

The intestate laws of virtually every state provide that the spouse and children get shares of the estate. The makeup of that split depends upon the state and number of children. If there are no children, then the surviving spouse may have to split the estate with the deceased's parents or siblings.

Problems created by intestacy

One of the real problems, as we see throughout this book, is the fact that minor children often inherit property. Unfortunately, or fortunately, minor children cannot *own* property. The mere fact that they are left part of your estate, under the watchful eye of the probate court, means that your spouse, or the guardian, might not be able to do what he/she wants. This puts quite a burden on that person. The following case illustrates much of what is bad about intestacy.

> *Robert Ellsworth died without a will (intestate). He left a wife, Betty, and four children, along with a home and some certificates of deposits (registered in his name alone). In Betty's state of residence, the rules stipulated that since she was just one of five remaining beneficiaries, she was only entitled to receive 20 percent of the intestate property. The remaining 80 percent was divided equally among her four daughters.*
>
> *Betty was appointed guardian of her children. The probate court had very definite limitations on what could be done with their share of the money. It could be invested only in government bonds or FDIC-insured accounts. If her children had needs that required large expenditures, she had to get the approval of the court, which in her county was difficult. In addition, she needed an attorney every time she went to court. She was also required to provide an annual accounting of the funds. Her late husband had promised her oldest daughter a car when she reached 16. The court said no. In fact, the court said no to many things.*
>
> *Early on, she thought about putting the daughters' shares of the home into her name in case she wanted to sell it. But her state laws required petitioning the court, advertising it and waiting a specified period of time. It also would have resulted in significant attorneys' fees. She couldn't afford to spend the money, so she decided not to change the title until the time came to sell.*

When that time came, her children's ages were 18 to 23. She went to each child and asked them to sign over their respective shares of the house. All agreed except the oldest child, Pat. She maintained that she was entitled to 20 percent of the proceeds of the house and refused to sign.

To make matters worse, Pat threatened to get an attorney and sue Betty for her share of the Social Security benefits that had been paid over the years. Betty had no choice but to give Pat 20 percent of the proceeds. They haven't spoken since.

This is but one tragic case illustrating how the lack of proper planning can be disastrous for the surviving family members. It illustrates but a few of the problems that can be caused by dying intestate.

Remember what was said in the preface: *We don't think we have a problem until we have a problem.* As long as Robert was alive, everything was fine. It didn't matter that he didn't have a will. How the house was owned was irrelevant. However, once his death occurred, the entire picture changed.

One of the purposes of estate planning is to ensure that your assets are distributed the way you want, not in some arbitrary manner. Dying intestate is like trying to walk through a mine field blindfolded. You might get to the other side, or you might get blown up along the way.

What is a will?

Back to the beginning. We all know what a will, or Last Will and Testament as it is officially titled, does. It is a written, properly witnessed and notarized document in which you express exactly how you want your property to pass. You also name an executor (or executrix if female) whose job is to make sure that your wishes are followed and that your property is disposed of as you want.

One confusing aspect of wills is that each state has its own complicated set of rules that must be precisely followed for a will to be valid. There are regulations concerning when and how the executor needs to be bonded, nominating guardians for minor or disabled children, laws of succession, disinheriting spouses and children, contesting wills, holographic (handwritten) wills, the effect of divorce, changes in the wills, etc. You should consult your attorney for information regarding your state.

Advantages of wills

Vehicle for passing property. A will gives you a means for passing your property to the people you want. You can leave your assets to a spouse, children, charity—virtually anyone you want. However, there are some limits. Different states have varying laws on the treatment of a spouse and children.

Can provide interim funds. In some states, a will can provide for interim funds for your family during probate. This can, to a limited extent, ensure that the family has money with which to pay their living expenses while the estate is in probate.

Care for minor children. A testamentary trust within the will can be used to care for minor children or to provide a stream of income for family members. Since children cannot own property (minor children are covered in Chapter 10), the trustmaker will name an individual or individuals (known as trustees) to handle the funds for the children's benefit. The remaining funds will be distributed to the children either at the age of majority or at the ages specified in the trust.

Reduce estate taxes. A properly drawn testamentary trust can help a married couple reduce estate taxes. Estate taxes are covered in detail in Chapters 6, 9 and 22.

Leave property to charity. A will can specify property to a charity or charitable organizations. Chapter 19 covers charitable remainder trusts, a preferred way for donating property.

Nominate guardians. A will allows you to name guardians to care for your minor children. If you have minor or disabled children, you need to ensure that the person of your choice will rear them. Without a will, this choice is in the hands of the court. Note, however, that while the court gives consideration to your preference, it is possible that you may be overruled.

> *Donna McGee was a divorcee with custody of her two children. Five years after she remarried, she was killed in an accident. In her will, she named her current husband as guardian of her minor children. However, her ex-husband wanted custody of his children.*

*His argument was that he was the natural father, and there was no
valid reason to deny him custody. The court agreed, and set aside the
desires of the mother.*

The courts try to give custody to the natural parent whenever possible. Even though the court may, for what it considers valid reasons,
go against your choice, you should still express your desires in your
will.

Inexpensive to prepare. As a rule, wills tend to be inexpensive to
prepare. I always get a kick out of picking up a paper when I'm
traveling around the country and seeing advertisements for low-cost
wills. I don't know how attorneys make a profit preparing wills for $50
or $100. There are some who say the only reason the attorney can af-
ford to do so is that he or she hopes to make up the loss by probating
the will. Different attorneys have told me different things, so I can
only guess each individual attorney's motive.

Disadvantages of a will

A will, however, has several disadvantages. But understand that
the following are not disadvantages compared to dying intestate, but
disadvantages compared with other types of planning that will be
discussed later.

Won't help in the case of your disability. Since a will only takes
effect upon your death, it can't take care of you during a period of disability. In this case, we are talking about a mental instability that
would preclude you from handling your own financial affairs. This is
discussed in detail in Chapter 23.

Guarantees probate. Contrary to what many people believe, a will
has to be probated, which can be time-consuming and costly. For a
married couple, it can mean two probates (covered in the next chapter). If you add two possible living probates, (discussed in Chapter 23),
you could end up with four probates.

Doesn't control all your property. A will usually doesn't control all
of your property. Certain holdings pass outside your will.

- **Jointly owned property** automatically passes to the other joint tenant, no matter what your will says.
- **Life insurance** automatically passes to the named beneficiary. The only way your will controls life insurance proceeds is if the beneficiary of the insurance is your estate.
- **Retirement plans** automatically pass to the named beneficiary. As with insurance, only retirement benefits payable to your estate pass according to your will.
- **Living trust** property passes according to the instructions in the trust, as covered in Chapters 7 and 8.

Takes your family public. Wills take your family public. If you have any doubt about this, just go down to your local probate court and review the wills on file. They are available to the media, the curious or anyone who might want to take advantage of circumstances.

> *Joanne and Roger Walker owned what they considered a modest farm. Over the years, they had purchased substantial equipment, thanks to their friendly banker. When Roger died, their banker became not-so-friendly. It seems the banker didn't have much confidence in Joanne's ability to continue the operation. With great reluctance, he called the loans. This made it necessary for Joanne to sell some equipment and land. However, because Roger's will was public, people interested in buying could go to the courthouse and learn the details of his finances. The result was that Joanne received only a fraction of the value and had to sell the bulk of the equipment and property to repay the banks. If the information hadn't been public, this might not have happened.*

Different interpretation in different states. Moving to another state can create problems. Although your will is probably valid in any state, its interpretation depends on the state where it is probated. What "share and share alike" means in Colorado may be different from what it means in Pennsylvania.

Easy to contest. Wills can easily be contested. The two D's, death and disability, seem to bring out the worst in people. I think it was Benjamin Franklin who said that you never really know what a person is like until you share an inheritance with him. We have all heard the horror stories of family members who have successfully contested a will. When a will is probated, the executor or executrix notifies potential heirs. This opens the door for a will contest. There are several grounds that can be used in contests, such as undue influence over the maker, improper execution, fraud, unsound mind, mental instability, etc. Typically, it is irrelevant whether the contest is valid. The rightful heirs, not wanting to take the time and money to fight a will contest, may settle just to get the matter concluded.

John and Elizabeth Benson had two sons, Chad and Randy. While Chad had given them no problems, Randy was always in trouble. In addition, he was extremely cruel to John and Elizabeth, to the point that they had ceased trying to continue a relationship with him. In their wills, they left virtually all their estate to Chad, with only 10 percent going to Randy. Upon their deaths, Randy contested the will. He said that his parents were unduly influenced by Chad and didn't understand what they were doing. He told Chad that he would tie up the estate in court for years if he didn't share a larger portion with him. Chad, not wanting to go through the time and expense of fighting his brother, agreed to give Randy 25 percent of the money.

What most people don't realize when it comes to a contested will is that the validity of the case is not necessarily relevant. The fact is that frequently, the rightful heirs settle only because it will be cheaper and less time-consuming.

Making your will more effective

There are several steps you can take to make sure your will doesn't come up against one of these planning problems.

Noncontest clause. You might consider a "noncontest" clause. This clause effectively eliminates an heir's inheritance if he or she contests the will. In spite of this, however, a probate judge can still allow the contest by ruling that the "noncontest" clause is "contrary to public policy."

Keep your will current. Throughout our lives, changes occur. Usually, people don't think to update their wills. But there are changes that need to be reflected in your will.

- Grown children become disabled. This can make it impossible for them to handle property.

- Divorce is rampant in this country. In some states a divorce invalidates a will. In others, it has no effect. In either case, the result is bad. In the first, property passes according to intestate laws. In the second, property can go to the ex-spouse.
- Children or other heirs die. This can, in some states, invalidate the will. At a minimum, it can result in changes in the distribution provisions.
- People move to different states. This can result in different interpretations of the will.
- Children are born. Again, this can require changes in distribution plans.
- The size and makeup of assets change. You may want to include more people in your will, or you may have to take into consideration estate taxes.
- Executors and guardians die. This will leave those important decisions up to the court.

You can handle these changes one of two ways: either by drawing up a new will or by adding a "codicil" amending your current will. Discuss this with your attorney to determine the best route for you.

Self-proving will. One of the inconvenient steps during probate is proving that a will is valid. This can involve having to contact those individuals who witnessed the will.

One way around this problem is with a self-proving will. In this case, when the original document is drafted, the testator (person who makes the will) and the witnesses also declare and sign before a notary public that they did, in fact, witness each other signing and witnessing the will. While this sounds a little convoluted, it should have the effect of preventing the time-consuming and costly process of dragging in the original witnesses. It boils down to taking a few extra minutes when the will is prepared to avoid possible major headaches for the executor later.

Careful choosing of executor. The natural tendency of most people is to pick his or her spouse to be the executor or executrix of the will. While this is the easiest, and initially least costly because it will save executor fees, it could cause problems down the road. The job of executor is not one to be taken lightly. An unsophisticated executor, one who has no business or financial experience, can be taken advantage of by someone during the probate process. This can result in unnecessary fees and expenses that milk the estate of valuable funds. While trying to save a few dollars in executor fees, thousands can be lost to inexperience.

Old wills interpreted under old laws. Before the Economic Recovery Tax Act of 1981 (ERTA), only one-half of your estate could be passed to your spouse estate tax-free. ERTA provided for the 100-percent marital deduction, under which you can pass 100 percent of your property estate tax-free to your spouse. However, if you have a will drafted prior to Sept. 13, 1981, chances are that it will be interpreted under the old rules. To remedy this potentially costly hazard, see your attorney and bring your estate plan up-to-date.

Conclusion

How do wills fulfill our definition of estate planning?

"During my life and after my death, I want to control and distribute my property in the manner I desire, minimizing all fees, taxes and court interference, preserving for myself, my family, and those I choose, the estate I have worked so hard to create."

Not too well, in my opinion. They alone don't take care of you during your life, they don't guarantee you can distribute your property as you want, and they certainly don't minimize fees and court interference.

Five

How Does the Probate System Work?

If there is one subject that has caused controversy in modern estate planning, it is probate. Many states have adopted the Uniform Probate Code, which made probate laws somewhat uniform in those states. Nevertheless, probate avoidance is still one of the main advantages expounded in the marketing of living trusts. "Avoid the Evils of Probate" shout the advertisements. And people, having heard of or personally experienced how bad probate can be, flock to these seminars.

What probate is

Probate is the process by which the debts of the deceased are paid, and the title to his or her property is changed to the heirs specified in the will. If there is no will, the property will pass according to state law. All property, other than that listed above, goes through probate, whether or not there is a will. This process is performed under the watchful eye of the probate judge, who may have been appointed or elected, and who may or may not have a law degree.

Is probate so bad?

That is the $64,000 question. If you listen to some doomsayers, it is terrible. If you listen to some advocates, there is nothing to it. Obviously, the truth lies somewhere in between. It depends on your jurisdiction, type of property you own, etc. Nevertheless, probate is only one issue in planning and should be viewed with all the other matters affecting your estate.

Assets avoiding probate

Before initiating our discussion of probate, let's review the assets that automatically avoid probate.

- Assets held in joint tenancy.
- Life insurance proceeds when they are paid to a named beneficiary and not to the estate of the deceased.
- Proceeds from a qualified retirement plan (pension, profit-sharing, IRAs, KEOGHs, SEPs, etc.) when the funds go directly to a named beneficiary.
- Property titled in a trust.

The parties

Although the probate judge presides over the process, your estate needs an executor (executrix, if female). This is the person you name responsible for handling the paperwork for the estate. If you have no will, the court will make this decision for you, as well as other decisions you have chosen not to make. The job of the executor or executrix is to get your estate to the point where it can be closed and your assets distributed. Of course, since you are working through the courts, the executor or executrix probably needs an attorney to help him or her. This can be costly.

The process

While the stated purpose of probate is to properly distribute the property of the deceased to the rightful parties, that is only the end result of an entire process. There is a chain of events that must occur first. The exact order of those events will depend upon the particular state.

Without going into great detail, the first thing that must be done is to *read and file the will*. This filing can be done immediately or at a convenient time. However, if an interested party (creditor, heir) is in a hurry, he or she can petition the court to begin the process. Otherwise, the executor/executrix will petition the court to have the will admitted. Once that is done, the process starts and the fun begins.

The executor/executrix must *inventory and appraise* the property. This is laborious at times because some property is difficult to value.

Additionally, people sometimes die with piles of old securities. Most times, obtaining the value is easy. Often, however, name changes or mergers can make it difficult. Most investment professionals know that US Steel is now USX Corporation, and International Harvester is Navistar. But many obscure companies have changed their names and have become difficult to trace.

While publicly traded stocks and bonds are the easiest to value, obtaining the value on privately held companies, where no active market exists, is extremely difficult. Medical practices, partnerships and business ventures are also difficult to value. (This is covered in Chapter 28.)

Newspaper notices in the local legal publication must be run to allow creditors and heirs the opportunity to file any claims they might have against the estate. This is the opportunity for disgruntled heirs to contest the will. The heirs and creditors have a certain time period (usually six months) to submit their claims and/or challenge the will. Talk about dragons!

The *validity* of the will must be ascertained. Each state has its own set of rules concerning the way a will must be drafted. It is at this point that it will be determined if those rules were properly followed. Was the will properly drafted? Was it duly witnessed? Is it, in fact, the last will, or are there others? Was the deceased of sound mind?

By now, all the inventories should be completed, valuations ascertained, creditors verified, disgruntled heirs heard. Although it might sound simple here, in some estates it can go on for years. Once this is completed, and assuming there are no problems, it is time to begin *settling the estate.*

Taxes and debts must be paid. There are income taxes that must be filed for both the deceased and his estate. It might be necessary to file estate tax returns.

A *final accounting* is filed with the court along with the executor/executrix's *petitions* to allow for final distribution. (What happens in the event property is left to a minor is covered in Chapter 10). Once accomplished, a *final discharge* can be obtained.

Advantages of probate

Court supervision. The court oversees the entire process and provides some protection to the heirs. Court approval must be secured before disbursements are made. Often, the executor/executrix must obtain a bond, thus providing the heirs some protection against dishonest acts by the representatives of the estate.

Court helps settle disputes. If there are disputes among the heirs, the court can serve to settle them. Earlier I said that probate is the perfect forum from which disgruntled heirs or family members can attack the will. If there are family members who feel they have been wronged, the probate court will resolve that dispute.

Limits time of claims against estate. Probate limits the time in which creditors can make claims against the estate. This can be especially important in the case of a doctor, because future malpractice claims can arise. Lack of proper planning can create a situation in which a suit filed years after your death leads to claims against your estate.

Postmortem planning. Postmortem (after death) tax planning techniques can be used since the estate is a separate taxpaying entity. Sometimes, there are opportunities for postponing income and moving it from one taxpaying entity to another.

Disadvantages of probate

Expense. It is a well-known fact that probate can be expensive. "Changing Times" reviewed a report prepared for AARP, which showed that legal fees often amount to 5 percent or more of an estate's value and sometimes exceed 20 percent. The report further revealed that fees "are often arbitrary, being only tenuously connected to the actual effort an attorney expends."

Time-consuming. Probate can also be time-consuming. The same AARP study said it takes a year or more, on average, to settle uncomplicated estates. A number of my clients wish their cases had been settled that quickly. Sometimes, it can drag on for many years.

Slows liquidation. The probate process can make it difficult to sell investments quickly. An executor wishing to sell stock or real estate in an estate must wait for court approval.

John Martin's father died September 20, 1987. His assets in-cluded a substantial stock portfolio that he had accumulated over the years. John, as executor of the estate, felt uncomfortable with so much invested in the stock market. He had recently liquidated his own portfolio and felt he should do the same in his father's estate. However, the probate process required a notification period that pre-cluded his liquidating any of the investments. When the stock market crashed on October 16, 1987, it severely reduced the value of the estate.

Public process. When a will is probated, the records are public in-formation, unless steps have been taken to avoid it. This means that anyone can go down to the courthouse and look at your will, see what you owned and to whom you were indebted, and take advantage of that situation. We saw the problems that created in the previous chapter.

Forum to contest. While the probate court can resolve disputes, the process also invites conflicts. Because you have to advertise, and the court provides the forum, you are inviting disgruntled heirs to contest the will. Although the contesting party may have no right to any of the money, the rightful heirs may settle rather than fight.

Lack of flexibility. There is a general lack of flexibility. For ex-ample, many courts limit how money under their jurisdictions may be invested, thus limiting potential returns. Another problem might occur when postmortem planning needs to be done, but is thwarted due to lack of knowledge by the judge or probate attorney.

Multiple probates. If you own property in different states, then you must go through probate in those states. If you are married, depend-ing upon how your property is owned, you may have to go through probate twice. And if you become disabled, that means even more probate. All of these can obviously be expensive propositions.

Conclusion

Being totally objective about probate is impossible. Opinions de-pend upon the persons to whom you are speaking and their biases. It also depends on their experiences...or how they earn their living.

Often, probate is not a problem at the death of the first spouse because most of the property is jointly titled or passes directly to a beneficiary, thus automatically avoiding probate. At the death of the second spouse, however, things can be different.

Nevertheless, the difficulty with probate is that it is the perfect example of "we don't think we have a problem until we have a problem." We have no idea how much of a problem probate might be until it's too late.

Again, look at our definition of estate planning.

"During my life and after my death, I want to control and distribute my property in the manner I desire, minimizing all fees, taxes and court interference, preserving for myself, my family, and those I choose, the estate I have worked so hard to create."

How does probate fit in? If you truly want your affairs to comply with that definition, then probate can be a definite hindrance. How much is something that will not be known until your death.

Personally, I have chosen to structure my estate to avoid probate. I prefer to keep my family and affairs out of court. But I also had other reasons for choosing the type of planning I did, and those are discussed in upcoming chapters.

Probate is just one part of the planning puzzle. Some people say that a little probate is no problem. Well, maybe a little cancer is no problem, also. But wouldn't we all like to avoid it if we could?

Six

How Do Estate Taxes Affect Me?

In 1992, Congress attempted to reduce the estate tax exemption. Fortunately, that attempt was turned back. But it's not over. It is reasonable to expect that the law could change within the next few years. The potential ramifications of any changes are discussed in Chapter 22. In the meantime, let's look at the rules as they stand today.

Uncle Sam has his ways. He gets you while you are alive, and he gets you when you're dead.

I think it was Will Rogers who said, "There are only two things in life that are certain: death and taxes. The only difference is that death doesn't get worse while Congress is in session!" It's only funny because it's true.

Taxes. Taxes. Taxes. I constantly meet with clients whose primary goal is to reduce taxes. But no matter how they try, they still pay more taxes. And it will get worse, as the '93 tax act proves.

And, then, the final insult: estate taxes. This is Uncle Sam's last shot. For you, estate taxes may or may not be a problem. But if they are, it could very well be that *you are worth only 45 to 65 percent of what you think you are worth.*

In spite of an estate tax that can take up to 55 percent of your assets (and more if pension excise, generation-skipping, and state inheritance taxes are included), it truly amazes me how few people have taken any meaningful steps to reduce those taxes. If you are in this boat, you are just throwing away hard-earned money.

Before going further, let's make sure you are up-to-date on the current law. Many aspects of this discussion involve U.S. citizens only.

Keep Uncle Sam From Devouring Your Life Savings

The rules

If you are *married,* you may leave $600,000 free of federal estate taxes to any person or combination of persons you want. In addition, you may pass an unlimited amount to your spouse federal estate tax-free (U.S. citizens only). No federal estate tax is due until the death of the surviving spouse.

If you are *single,* you may pass $600,000 free from federal estate taxes to any person or combination of persons you want.

Of course, although there is an unlimited marital deduction, your estate does get taxed when the surviving spouse dies. So while it's not a free ride, it is an improvement over the previous law.

Although the government refers to it as a "federal estate tax," I call it a "federal confiscation tax." After all, that's what they're doing. They are confiscating money that has already been taxed...several times. You paid tax when you earned it, you paid tax when you invested it and earned interest, and now they want to tax it again.

Calculating your estate

Most people assume they don't have an estate tax problem, so they never consider it. Nevertheless, it is important to determine for sure whether your estate is facing any potential taxes, especially in light of possible changes. The first step is to determine the makeup of your estate. What does Uncle Sam include and exclude in determining the value of your estate? Let's look.

Step 1. Add the value of the following assets:

a. Your home.
b. Securities (stock, bonds, etc.).
c. Real estate.
d. Retirement plan.
e. Bank accounts (savings, CDs, checking).
f. Life insurance you own.
g. Your business interests.

h. Personal property (jewelry, furnishings, automobiles, boats, etc.).
i. Accounts and/or notes receivable.
j Jointly owned property.
k. Investments held in custodial accounts for minors
l. Property located outside the United States.
m. Partnership interests.
n. Other assets.

Step 2. From this figure, deduct the following:

a. Accounts and loans payable.
b. Mortgages payable.
c. Funeral and administrative expenses.
d. Liens against property.
e. Unpaid taxes.
f. Other liabilities.

Step 3. This figure represents your **adjusted gross estate**.

Step 4. From this figure, you deduct the following:

a. Marital deduction.
b. Charitable deductions.

Step 5. This figures represents your **taxable estate**.

If you leave everything to your spouse, then your entire *adjusted gross estate* will be deducted as the marital deduction in 4(a) above. As a result, your *taxable estate* will be zero, as will your taxes.

If you are not married, or if you are the second spouse to die, then we must continue the calculation. It can get complicated with regard to various credits and adjusted taxable gifts, so we will assume that you have nothing that would further adjust your estate or taxes.

Step 6. Compute your *gross federal estate tax* using the following table. (These are the federal estate and gift tax rates until 1993. They change at that point.) Any state inheritance taxes are in addition to these figures.

Taxable Estate	Tax Owed	Plus %	On Amount
$0-10,000	0	18	0
10,001-20,000	1,800	20	10,000
20,001-40,000	3,800	22	20,000
40,001-60,000	8,200	24	40,000
60,001-80,000	13,000	26	60,000
80,001-100,000	18,200	28	80,000
100,001-150,000	23,800	30	100,000
150,001-250,000	38,800	32	150,000
250,001-500,000	70,800	34	250,000
500,001-750,000	155,800	37	500,000
750,001-1,000,000	248,300	39	750,000
1,000,001-1,250,000	345,800	41	1,000,000
1,250,001-1,500,000	448,300	43	1,250,000
1,500,001-2,000,000	555,800	45	1,500,000
2,000,001-2,500,000	780,800	49	2,000,000
2,500,001-3,000,000	1,025,800	53	2,500,000
3,000,001-10,000,000	1,290,800	55	3,000,000
10,000,001-21,040,000	$5,140,800	60	10,000,000
over $21,040,001	$11,764,800	55	$21,040,000

Note: The purpose of the 60-percent tax from $10 million to $21.040 million is to eliminate the benefit of the unified credit for those estates. In other words, on estates over $21.04 million, there is no $600,000 exemption.

Step 7. From that figure (your gross estate tax), subtract the unified credit of $192,800. Remember, earlier we said you can pass $600,000 free of estate taxes. The figure $192,800 is the amount of tax on that $600,000 transfer. So while it is said everyone has a $600,000 exemption, what they really have is a $192,800 tax credit. That is why we call the $600,000 a credit equivalent or exemption equivalent rather than an exemption.

However, for easier reading, we will refer to the $600,000 credit equivalent and $192,800 tax credit as a $600,000 exemption.

Although the chart shows that estate tax rates start at 18 percent, because of the way the $192,800 tax credit is calculated, the first dollars over $600,000 are actually taxed at 37 percent. That means that when your taxable estate gets above $600,000, the excess is taxed at 37 percent or higher!

To review, you have two tax breaks: the unlimited marital deduction, by which you can leave an unlimited amount of property to your spouse; and, currently, a $600,000 exemption, by which you can leave that amount to any other person or persons. However, it takes special planning to take advantage of both breaks.

Traditional planning

Unfortunately, in the most cases, the couple's estate has not been structured to take advantage of the first-to-die's $600,000 exemption. Instead, the husband has left everything to the wife, and vice versa. If this is the way your estate is structured, you will lose your $600,000 exemption, and this can result in substantial, unnecessary estate taxes.

Let's look at some numbers and see what we're talking about.

Donald Purcell was 48, his wife Rebecca was 46. They had three children, ages 21, 18 and 16. They had a total net estate of $2 million, including the value of their home, stocks and bonds, retirement plans, personal property, his business, his life insurance and the custodial accounts they had established for their minor child. They each had simple wills leaving their assets to each other, if living, otherwise to their children. They each owned one-half the assets. He died in an automobile accident. She died a week later from injuries sustained in the same accident.

Calculating the tax (Exhibit 1)

Let's calculate the estate taxes on the Purcell's estate.

- Mr. Purcell's adjusted gross estate was $980,000 after probate and administrative expenses of 2 percent.
- There was no tax at Mr. Purcell's death since everything went to his wife under the unlimited marital deduction.
- Mrs. Purcell's adjusted gross estate was $1,940,400. This consisted of her $1 million, plus her husband's $980,000, less 2 percent expenses.

- The gross estate tax on the $1,940,400 (after the deductible expenses) estate that Mrs. Purcell left was $753,980.
- After her $192,800 tax credit (the amount of tax on her $600,000 exemption), the estate taxes were $561,180.

Their children received $1,379,220. The estate tax return was filed. The children paid $561,180 in taxes to Uncle Sam within nine months, all in cash. As a result, only $1,379,220 passed to their heirs. In this case, it didn't matter who died first or how the assets were divided. The results would have been the same.

The Purcells structured their estate the way most couples do. The first to die leaves all of his or her property to the spouse under the unlimited marital deduction. As a result, he or she never uses, and thus loses, his or her $600,000 exemption. This means that at the death of the surviving spouse, the heirs must pay more estate taxes than would have been necessary with proper planning. This alternative planning is discussed in Chapter 9.

State inheritance taxes

Besides federal estate taxes, your heirs may have to pay state inheritance taxes. Generally, there are two ways that states handle inheritance taxes.

Approximately half the states are called "federal credit" states. They receive part of the federal estate taxes you pay, but have no inheritance tax of their own. Thus, by using the estate tax schedule printed in this chapter, you can calculate your total estate taxes.

The balance of the states have some form of "inheritance tax" in addition to the federal estate tax. Therefore, you can assume that you must pay more in total estate and inheritance taxes than is reflected in the schedule. Included in this taxing group are Connecticut, Delaware, Indiana, Iowa, Kansas, Kentucky, Louisiana, Maryland, Massachusetts, Mississippi, Nebraska, New York, North Carolina, Ohio, Oklahoma, Pennsylvania, South Dakota and Tennessee. Since the rules for each taxing state are different, and constantly changing, it is impossible to include all the rules for each state in this book.

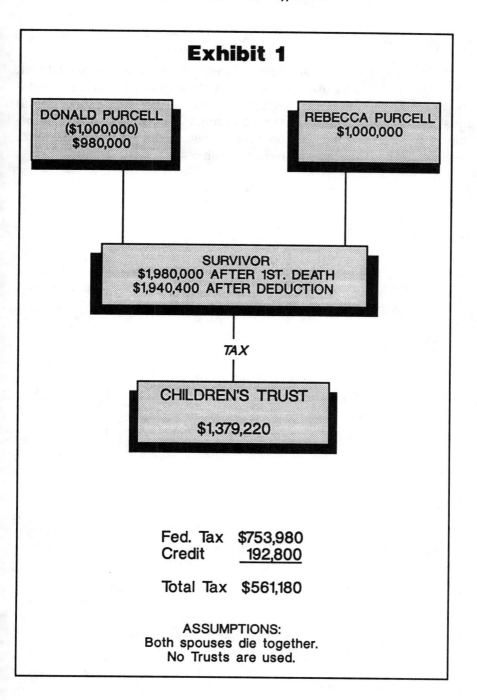

Exhibit 1

DONALD PURCELL
($1,000,000)
$980,000

REBECCA PURCELL
$1,000,000

SURVIVOR
$1,980,000 AFTER 1ST. DEATH
$1,940,400 AFTER DEDUCTION

TAX

CHILDREN'S TRUST

$1,379,220

Fed. Tax $753,980
Credit   192,800

Total Tax $561,180

ASSUMPTIONS:
Both spouses die together.
No Trusts are used.

Conclusion

Estate taxes are usually ignored because most people don't think they have a problem. And while this is statistically true (only a relatively small percentage of estates do have to pay estate taxes), you must include this as part of your planning. We will see in the following chapters that when you do have an estate tax problem, there are various methods to help you reduce these costs.

Part II

Controlling
Your Estate

Seven

What is a Revocable Living Trust?

We have looked at the traditional forms of planning. I have discussed methods of ownership and the potential problems they create. I have covered wills and probate. And, I emphasized the estate tax problem. Now let's move to a unique form of planning that can help solve many problems that have been raised: the *revocable living trust*.

Plan for the best?

In estate planning, as in life, most people live their lives hoping for the best. This is what I call the "Ostrich Syndrome." They bury their heads in the sand and hope bad things won't happen. This thinking is a blueprint for disaster.

Does Apple design a computer and hope it will work? Does Boeing design an airplane, sell it to USAir without testing, and hope it will fly? Of course not! So why does it make any more sense to hope everything will work out with your estate? Hope you won't die while your children are minors? Hope you and your joint tenant won't die together? Hope that probate won't be a problem? Hope nobody will contest your will? Hope you won't become disabled?

Things go wrong every day. You are probably familiar with Murphy's Law: "Anything that can go wrong will go wrong." Remember the dragons. They are just waiting to pounce on your estate.

Anticipate the problems

Proper planning means that you must anticipate potential problems and take the necessary steps *in advance* to avoid them. In my

56

experience, very few people do this. Most do nothing at all. The rest use traditional planning methods and hope things will work out. If you are going to plan at all, doesn't it make sense to do it right the first time and eliminate the potential problems and hassles before they occur? I think so. And one of the best tools to accomplish this is the *inter vivos* trust, better known as the revocable living trust.

When you mention trusts, many people think of this scene in the old movies: An 80-year-old widow is begging her banker to give her some money from the trust fund that was established for her. Scary, isn't it? Thankfully, that is not what we're talking about here. This modern type of trust allows *you* to maintain complete control over *your* property as long as *you* choose.

Why wills are emphasized

Although most people think that wills are old and trusts are new, the opposite is true. Wills are relatively new while trusts have been around for longer than most of us realize. Nevertheless, wills have been the favored method of passing property. Some say this is because attorneys like the fees that probate generates. Others say that law schools tend to emphasize wills rather than trusts.

I like to think it's the latter case. I hate to think that attorneys recommend wills because of the money they will eventually make from probate. But I have heard of attorneys who brag about the wills they have in their filing cabinets, waiting for clients' families to come in to probate those wills. Some call this their "guaranteed annuity."

Definition of a trust

A trust is like a legal box that holds assets. Within the trust, there are three parties:

1. The trustmaker (also called the settlor or grantor).
2. The trustees.
3. The beneficiaries.

The *trustmaker*, or grantor, is the person or persons who create the trust and transfer his and/or her assets into it. The *trustees* are the people who manage the trust. The *beneficiaries* are the people who benefit from the trust.

Setting up the trust

Setting up a trust is not difficult, but there are important decisions that you must make. In the following chapters, we will discuss choosing trustees and distributing the funds. At this point, let's look at the basics of a living trust.

The beauty of the living trust is that you can name yourself (and/or your spouse) as initial trustees of your own trust. As such, you have complete control over your trust and the property in it. You can add or sell property, amend or revoke the trust. You will probably name yourself (and/or your spouse) lifetime beneficiaries of the trust. As trustee, you can do whatever is necessary to take care of you, the beneficiary.

> *After much discussion with their attorney, Robert and Mary Jones decided to establish a revocable living trust. Their attorney drafted the document, and it was duly signed and notarized. Mr. and Mrs. Jones then transferred their assets into the trust. Did they have to transfer all their assets in the trust? No. They could have put in as many or as few of their assets as they wanted. Some assets, such as professional corporation stock, normally can't be owned by a trust. But, the Joneses, for reasons we will see shortly, decided to transfer all their assets into the trust.*
>
> *Mr. and Mrs. Jones wanted to maintain control over the assets in the trust. Since they didn't want a third party involved, they named themselves as trustees. As trustees, they can do whatever is necessary to follow the guidelines they have set up for the beneficiaries. Who are the beneficiaries? Mr. and Mrs. Jones. It is for their benefit that the trust was established. In other words, they set up the trust, they control the assets in the trust, and they benefit from it. They hold all three positions.*

The Joneses didn't have to occupy all three positions (trust-makers, trustees, beneficiaries). They could have named a financial institution, a relative or any third party of their choice as trustee. They didn't have to be the beneficiaries. They could have named their children, their parents or anyone they chose as beneficiaries.

A living trust has a great deal of flexibility. In fact, there are only two major limitations. First, the trust cannot contain illegal provisions. Second, the trust cannot last forever. The "rule against perpetuities" limits the length of time a trust may remain in effect. This law is designed to keep the super-wealthy from passing assets from generation to generation without taxation. The only exception to this rule is if the beneficiary is a qualified charity.

Transferring property into the trust

For a variety of reasons, as we will see shortly, you will want to title your property in the name of the trust. For example, in the case of Mr. and Mrs. Jones, their trust was titled:

"Robert C. Jones and Mary F. Jones, trustees, or their successors in trust, under the Robert C. and Mary F. Jones Living trust, dated February 4, 1994."

The ways to transfer property are covered in Chapter 14.

Advantages of a living trust

Takes care of you while you are alive. Unlike a will, which doesn't become effective until you die, a living trust contains provisions to provide for you during your life. In the event of a disability that keeps you from handling your financial affairs, the successor trustee(s) you have named can handle your financial affairs without going through any court procedures. This is covered in Chapter 23.

You name your own trustees. You can name your own trustees. The initial trustees can and probably will be you and your spouse. If either of you becomes unable to handle your financial affairs because of death or disability, the other spouse can automatically take over. If your spouse is unable to carry on, the successor trustees you named in your trust will carry on. This is certainly better than going to probate court and having a guardian or custodian named.

Avoids probate. Property titled in the name of a living trust avoids probate. For example, if your home is titled in the name of your trust, it will pass to your beneficiary probate-free. This can be quite an advantage. No matter what you may feel about probate, it appears to me that avoiding it is preferable to the cost and time delays.

Avoids multiple probates. If you own property in several states, you must go through probate in each of those states. Since a living trust avoids all probate (if the property is titled in the name of the trust), it can eliminate probate expenses and time delays. In addition, it will eliminate the need to probate the same property more than once.

Foster Markle owned 50 acres of land in his own name. Upon his death, it passed to his wife via his will. This was the first probate. Upon Mrs. Markle's death, the property will go through probate again.

Leave your own instructions. Your trust will contain your own special instructions for your trustees. You have the opportunity to leave unlimited, detailed instructions concerning how you want to be cared for in the event of your disability, and how you want your loved ones cared for upon your death. Since this is one of the primary advantages of a living trust, make sure that your attorney drafts the document to your specification and that it includes all your instructions.

Hard to contest. Unlike a will, which provides a forum for disgruntled heirs to contest, a living trust is very difficult to overturn. Remember our case from the chapter on wills:

John and Elizabeth Benson had two sons, Chad and Randy. While Chad had given them no problems, Randy was always in trouble. In addition, he was extremely cruel to John and Elizabeth, to the point that they had ceased trying to continue a relationship with him. In their wills, they left virtually all their estate to Chad, with only 10 percent going to Randy. Upon their deaths, Randy contested the will. He said that his parents were unduly influenced by Chad and didn't understand what they were doing. He told Chad that he would tie up the estate in court for years if he didn't share a larger portion with him. Chad, not wanting to go through the time and expense of fighting his brother, agreed to give Randy 25 percent of the money.

This scenario would have been difficult with a living trust for three reasons.

1. With a living trust, the assets are distributed to the beneficiaries almost immediately. It would have been of little or

no value for Randy to threaten Chad, because Chad would have already received his share of the money. He would have had to sue Chad in court, and based on historical precedent, Randy would have lost.

2. The living trust would have contained a "noncontest" clause. This would have stated that if any beneficiary were to contest the trust, he or she would receive nothing. Therefore, by contesting the trust, Randy would probably have lost even that amount to which he was entitled.

3. With a living trust, the argument of incompetency or lapsed memory is difficult to use. John and Elizabeth would have worked with the trust constantly. Every bank and brokerage statement they received would have been sent to them as trustees. They would have received money and paid bills as trustees. They couldn't have been incompetent and done all that. Unlike a will, which is usually filed away and never reviewed, they would have worked with the trust constantly. John and Elizabeth would have been very much aware of the provisions of the trust.

Care for minor children. Your trust is a vehicle to take care of your minor children. In the "pour-over" will, you name a guardian to care for the children. In your trust, you name a trustee (or trustees) to take care of the financial affairs of the children. Therefore, you can have two different people watching the children and watching each other for the benefit of the children. The kids and guardians stay out of probate court. They are provided for in the manner you desire. You can instruct the trustee, if you desire, to provide funds for special situations, such as private schooling, a wedding, special education, etc. You can provide instructions for distributing the money at the ages you desire. Chapter 10 provides a discussion of caring for minor children.

Instead of a living will, you can include a trust in your will. This is a "testamentary" trust, and it is activated upon your death. If you feel more comfortable within the confines of the probate court, then this would be an option. If you would rather not involve the court, then a living trust would make more sense. Chapter 12 contains a comparison of both types of trusts.

Reduce estate taxes. Properly drawn, your trust can help reduce your estate taxes *if you are married* and if you have not previously used your $600,000 exemption. This is covered in detail in Chapter 9. This same savings can be realized through the use of a testamentary trust in a will, but it will go through probate. Additionally, it can be accomplished by leaving property outright to a person other than your spouse.

Avoid lawsuit problems. A properly drafted living trust, under the right circumstances, can be helpful in avoiding the problems of a lawsuit. This subject is covered in Chapter 27 by attorney Kelly Burke.

No time delays. Unlike a will, which must go through the probate process, the use of a living trust allows the beneficiaries to receive money and assets immediately.

No additional or separate income tax returns. When a living trust is established, your income tax situation does not change. On trusts created after 1980, as long as you are trustee of your own trust, and as long as all the trust's assets are in the United States, you do *not* have to file a Form 1041. Instead, you report your income on your Form 1040 (or 1040A), just as you do now. There are no extra taxes to pay, no new forms to file, no separate taxpayer identification number. You are not beating the IRS out of any income taxes. Everything stays the same. Upon your death, depending upon the disposition of the assets, there can be additional tax forms. On trusts created before 1980, you have the option of reporting the income either way: on a 1040 or 1041.

Keep affairs private. A living trust keeps your personal finances private upon your death. Unlike a will, which is public record, your living trust is totally private—nobody will know your business unless your trustees choose to disclose it. There are times when a party with whom you are dealing, such as a stock brokerage firm, will need documentation verifying the existence of the trust and your powers as trustee. In these cases, it is not necessary to provide the entire document. Rather, give them an "Affidavit of trust," which certifies the trust's validity and contain copies of those portions of the trust they need.

Can change the terms. You can easily change the terms of the trust during your lifetime. Remember, it is a *revocable* trust. That means that while you (the trustmaker) are alive, you can change the terms or can revoke the trust entirely.

Don't need to amend to change property. A question that always arises is, "Do I have to change my trust every time I buy or sell property?" No, you do not. Your property is titled in the name of your trust. If you sell your home, you sell it as trustee of the trust. If you buy a new home, you title it in the name of the trust. It works like IBM. Every time they buy a new building, they don't change their corporate charter. The title is evidence of their ownership. Your trust works the same way. You can move your CDs, change your brokerage account and buy and sell securities. None of these requires a change in your trust.

No ongoing fees. As long as you remain trustee of your own trust, there are no continuing fees. The only cost is to establish the trust. From then on, the only additional costs would be if you need to change the terms of the trust. These changes usually take two forms: changing the trustees and changing the distribution provisions of the trust. The former can be avoided by naming sufficient successor trustees. Changing the distribution of property usually involves changing how children will receive the money upon the death of you and your spouse.

Disadvantages of a living trust

Cost. Living trusts are *initially* more expensive than wills. We have all seen advertisements for will preparation for $50 or $100. Trusts, on the other hand, can cost anywhere from $500 to $2,000 depending on the attorney and the work involved.

Cost, however, is a very difficult subject to quantify. How, for example, do you put a price on keeping affairs private, taking care of yourself and your family in the case of your disability or death, saving the time and cost of probate, taking care of your minor children, etc.?

You can't. So you can't just compare the cost of wills and trusts. You are dealing with too many unknowns. You really have no idea what your heirs are going to need to handle your estate because we don't think we have a problem until we have a problem. You don't know how many dragons might pop up. Again, it comes to planning. Are you planning for the best or planning for the worst? If it is the latter, then cost is not a significant factor.

One last factor concerning cost: If cost weren't a factor, most people (although probably not most attorneys) would agree that a living trust is more advantageous than a will. Therefore, the discussion is not necessarily whether a trust is better than a will; the question is whether a trust is worth the initial cost. This is discussed in Chapter 13.

Lose court supervision. One of the disadvantages of a living trust is the opposite of one of the advantages—avoiding probate. While you avoid probate with a living trust, you also lose the court supervision. Since you are giving your trustee the power to do all these good things, it is possible that he or she might do something that is not in the best interest of the beneficiaries. With a trust, you lose some protection since the court is not overseeing the trustee. However, if you think this might be a problem, one way around it is to name co-trustees, such as a relative, friend or trust department of a local bank.

Must transfer property into trust. As stated previously, if you are going to avoid probate with the living trust, your property must be titled in the name of the trust. Many people try to save attorneys' fees by purchasing a book that includes all the forms necessary to do a trust. One of the many problems with doing this is that you may not follow through with the complete process, which includes transferring property into the trust. This is an integral part of the process and must be accomplished in order to realize full benefit. But if you think that transferring property is difficult when you are alive, think how much more difficult it will be after your death. Transferring property is discussed in detail in Chapter 14.

No unique tax savings method. There are two types of taxes with which we concern ourselves in planning: income taxes and estate taxes. While a trust doesn't save any income taxes, it can be a big advantage when it comes to estate taxes—if you haven't previously used your $600,000 exemption. (Chapter 9 includes a full discussion of saving estate taxes with a trust.) It is important to note, however, that the same estate tax savings can be obtained whether you use a testamentary trust in a will or a revocable living trust.

But remember our previous discussion of cost. Whereas a will is inexpensive and a living trust can run into higher dollars, a testamentary trust falls somewhere in between. Obviously, because of the additional work involved, the attorney must charge more than he or she would for the standard will. But, don't forget, the testamentary trust must go through probate, and that has some disadvantages.

Need a competent attorney. I hesitate to include this. It's the same as saying that one disadvantage of surgery is that you need a competent surgeon. While it seems obvious in medicine, it's not so obvious in law. There are some attorneys who attempt to practice in areas in which they are not totally qualified. This can be disastrous for you. It is your duty to make sure that the attorney who does your estate planning work specializes in that area and can do good work.

Doesn't cut off time of creditors. A living trust, by avoiding the probate process, loses one of the advantages of probate: cutting the time in which creditors can attempt to get funds from the estate. Although this affects only a small number of people, it can be a concern to people who fear a lawsuit after their deaths. That is why, in planning with certain professionals, it is recommended that a small amount of property be left to go through probate with proper notification to the creditors. This can be done either by leaving some assets out of the trust to go through probate, or by having the executor open a probate estate after your death.

Lack of understanding by advisors. One of the biggest problems in working with living trusts is the fact that most attorneys and advisors either don't understand them or don't want to learn about them. Shop around until you find someone who is willing to work with you.

Lack of understanding by institutions. In addition to the advisors who don't understand them, you may run into employees of banks and brokerage firms who are not familiar with how to handle trust accounts. Although rare with brokerage firms who work with trust accounts daily, this occurs more often with banks. Many people go into a bank to change an account, and the person to whom they are talking has no idea what to do. One of the reasons for this is the natural turnover of people. Nevertheless, the manager should be familiar with trusts and can help.

Comparing advantages with disadvantages

Comparing advantages and disadvantages is never easy. Certainly, you can't base your decision solely on the number of each. You must look at your particular situation and decide whether the advantages offset the disadvantages. That is why you need to work with a competent estate planning team. Everyone's situation is different. You must consider the advantages in light of those factors that are important to you based upon your goals and priorities. The same is true with the disadvantages. You may look at the disadvantages and see no problems. On the other hand, there may be a few factors that concern you. Remember what I said earlier: This is *your* estate and *your* plan. You must ensure that the plan is designed for your needs and nobody else's.

Conclusion

I have seen the results of death or disability with and without a living trust. Those distinct differences make me a believer in the benefits of the revocable living trust in the right situation. Again, I must emphasize the words *in the right situation.* Nevertheless, the living trust, more than the other planning methods, appears to fulfill the terms of our definition.

> *"During my life and after my death, I want to control and distribute my property in the manner I desire, minimizing all fees, taxes and court interference, preserving for myself, my family, and those I choose, the estate I have worked so hard to create."*

- Does the living trust work during your life and after your death? *Yes.*

- Does the living trust allow you to control and distribute your property in the manner you desire? *Yes.*

- Does the living trust help you minimize all fees? Except for the initial cost? *Yes.*

- Does the living trust help you minimize taxes? *Yes.*

- Does the living trust minimize court interference? *Yes.*

- Does the living trust help you preserve your estate for yourself, your family, and those you choose? *Yes.*

That said, how do you know that you need a living trust? In Chapter 13 we will review the ways of determining if a living trust is for you and work to separate rhetoric from reality.

Eight

What Are the Ways of Structuring a Living Trust?

The beauty of a living trust is that it can be structured to your specifications. Done properly, designing a living trust is like building a home. In the latter case, you hire an architect to draw up the plans, but you dictate the basics: number of levels, bedrooms, baths, pool, decks, etc. But no matter what you want, the architect must stay within certain guidelines. It will have a roof, walls, floor, electricity, running water, indoor plumbing, meet restrictive covenants, etc.

The same is true with your living trust. While it must also stay within certain legal guidelines, it will reflect your concern for your family and contain your instructions for caring for them.

While this is neither a do-it-yourself book nor a guide to structuring a living trust, it is important to get an overview of the process. We will look at how to live with a living trust in Chapter 14. At this point, we are only covering the basic decisions you need to make so you can receive maximum benefit from your trust.

Decisions that must be made

There are four general decisions you must consider.

1. Do you want **joint** or **separate** trusts?
2. Who will be the **trustees**? These are the people who will carry forth your instructions both during your life and after your death.

3. How will you provide for yourself and your spouse as **lifetime beneficiaries**?
4. How do you want your money distributed to the **ultimate beneficiaries** upon the deaths of yourself and your spouse?

If you are single, you will obviously establish a separate trust. If you are married, you can either set up a joint trust for you and your spouse, or you can establish a separate trust for each of you. Which you choose depends upon your personal situation. Let's look at how this determination can be made.

Joint trust

A joint trust is similar to joint tenancy. Both spouses are usually the joint trustees and together control the property. For most people, this is the most comfortable way of handling their assets because it is familiar. It is also convenient because there is only one trust document and one set of paperwork. A joint trust is used successfully in community property states as a means of holding property.

Separate trusts

There are occasions when a married couple will use separate trusts.

- They have children by previous marriages and want to ensure that their respective children receive their just inheritance.
- A doctor or businessperson is concerned about the exposure of a lawsuit. The couple may put the bulk of their assets in the trust of the nonexposed spouse, thus protecting their wealth. For a detailed discussion, see Chapter 27.
- They have entered into their marriage with separate property that they, for personal reasons, would like to keep that way. Second marriages are discussed in Chapter 30.

The ultimate decision you make will be dependent upon your particular situation. While I have reviewed each method, there are distinct advantages and disadvantages that you should discuss with your attorney.

Choosing trustees

The next decision you need to make is selecting your trustees. As a rule, you will name trustees to serve in the following capacity.

Initial trustees are those people who are the trustees the day the trust is established. If you are the trustmaker, you can name anyone you desire as the trustee. *Most likely you will name yourself and/or your spouse as initial trustees or co-trustees.* As trustees, you have the same control over the property as you do when it is in your own name. You can buy it, sell it, gift it, pledge it—anything you want to do—as long as it conforms to the rules of the trust and is for the welfare of the beneficiaries (most likely you and your spouse). If you are single, you can be the sole trustee. On the other hand, you can name any other person or financial institution as sole or co-trustee. For example, some older people name their children as trustees or co-trustees.

Disability trustees are those people whom you appoint to take care of you in the event of your mental or physical incapacity. In a trust, disability is not a broken leg or a crushed hand. It is anything that will keep you from handling your own financial affairs. *While most people name their spouse as trustee,* the option is yours.

Death trustees are those people whom you appoint to take care of the beneficiaries in the event of your death. *Again, the surviving spouse might be the sole trustee, or you may name co-trustees.* If there isn't a surviving spouse, then you can name any other person or persons as death trustees.

As you can see, you and/or your spouse can hold all trustee positions, assuming you are able. This feature of control is what makes living trusts so popular.

I like to see people list at least four successor trustees in the event one or more cannot serve. It is inevitable that circumstances will keep a trustee from serving. By making necessary arrangements in advance, it will save time and expense down the road.

How to choose

Choosing your trustees can be one of the most difficult aspects of setting up your living trust. Trustees have a lot of power. They are going to be handling your money and following your instructions on caring for you and your family. Therefore, you must have full confidence that they will do their jobs. You want trustees who think like you and share your values. You want people who care about you and will be concerned for the welfare of your family.

It is understood that your primary concern should be the trustworthiness of the trustees. One of the advantages of a living trust is its freedom from court supervision. That could quickly turn into a disadvantage with the wrong trustee.

It is possible that the trustee could defraud the beneficiaries of their money. Although you can require the trustee to furnish annual statements to the beneficiaries, if the latter are minors or disabled, the reports will be of little value. If you have any concern that this might happen, then consider having joint trustees, such as two individuals, an individual and a bank, or just a bank.

Financial institutions as trustees

Speaking of banks, there are occasions when you might want a trustee with more experience and stability than a family member can provide. Some people feel uncomfortable naming a child as the sole trustee, no matter what the age. Therefore, the use of a financial institution as a sole or co-trustee might make sense.

There are several advantages to using a trust department of a commercial bank as trustee. They are insured against illegal acts by employees—you don't have to worry about them running off with the money like Uncle Joe. They are experienced in handling trust affairs. They have the expertise to handle your investment dollars.

There are also several disadvantages. There is the cost of managing the trust, which usually averages 1 percent per year. Banks tend to be impersonal. They change personnel frequently. And in some cases, their investment experience has been less than stellar.

However, nobody is perfect. Banks do make excellent co-trustees, and it can make sense to use them in this capacity. When coupled with a relative, a financial institution may serve your purpose well. If you feel the need for a commercial fiduciary, talk with a few trust officers and choose an institution with which you feel comfortable.

Obligation of the trustees

The obligation of your trustees is as strong as the law: They have the fiduciary duty of following your instructions as set forth in your trust. This is a responsibility that, when handled properly, can make life easier for you and your family.

John and Mary Richards set up a living trust naming themselves as initial trustees. They each listed their choice of successor trustees as follows:

John: Disability trustees

1. Mary, wife
2. Sue and Bob, children
3. Jack, brother
4. Kathy, sister
5. First National Bank

Mary: Disability trustees

1. John, husband
2. Sue and Bob, children
3. Carole, sister
4. Janet, sister
5. First National Bank

John suffered a stroke and became partially paralyzed. Following the rules of their trust, Mary became sole trustee. She did not have to take John through "living probate," the process by which she would be appointed guardian (discussed in Chapter 23). She didn't need the services of an attorney. She just followed the instructions contained in the trust.

If Mary becomes disabled, then their children, Sue and Bob, become co-trustees and will take care of their parents per the trust. If Sue and Bob cannot serve, then the successors listed in the trust will follow. In any case, no living probate is necessary.

John and Mary named the following trustees in the event of their deaths:

John: Death trustees

1. Mary, wife
2. Sue, Al and Bob
3. Jack, brother
4. Kathy, sister
5. First National Bank

Mary: Death trustees

1. John, husband
2. Sue, Al and Bob, children
3. Carole, sister
4. Janet, sister
5. First National Bank

When John dies, Mary can take over without missing a beat. Because their property is titled in the trust, no probate will be necessary. There will be no expenses and no delays. Mary will be able to handle everything herself.

The disability and death trustees can be identical or different. In this case, the Richards felt most comfortable with Sue and Bob taking care of their affairs in the event of their disability but didn't want their youngest son, Al, involved in this aspect. However they did want all three working together upon their deaths. That way, none of the children would feel left out. Additionally, they each named different people as successors after their children. Their thinking was that if the spouse and children were not around, they would like their own relatives caring for them.

Conclusion

A primary advantage of a trust is that it allows you to choose those people whom you want to handle your financial affairs. Whether those people are relatives, friends or a financial institution, it takes some thought and planning.

Nine

How Can I Save Estate Taxes and Care for My Family?

The next decision to be considered is how you want to use the trust to take care of your family upon your death. In addition, if you have an estate tax problem, you want to consider how, at the same time, you can reduce the eventual estate tax liability of your heirs.

Previously we saw how to calculate estate taxes and looked at the case of Donald and Rebecca Purcell, whose children had to pay over $561,000 in estate taxes. One of the purposes of this book is to help you reduce the cost of your estate taxes. So let's take our first step toward that goal by examining the use of a living trust. *If you don't have an estate tax problem (you're married with an estate under $600,000 or you are single and can't use a trust to reduce your taxes), just concentrate on the structuring aspects and ignore the numbers.* While you can use either a testamentary trust (part of a will) or a revocable living trust to reduce estate taxes, we will concentrate on the living trust.

The $600,000 exemption

Remember from our previous discussion that most married people, at their deaths, leave all their property directly to their spouse. As a result, the heirs lose the advantage of the first-to-die's $600,000 exemption. One of the purposes of estate planning is to capture this.

It can be captured one of two ways: Property can be left outright to another person or persons (totaling not more than $600,000), or property can be left directly to a family trust (also called credit or by-pass trust). In either case, the property is removed from the estate of both spouses, thus reducing future estate taxes on the death of the surviving spouse.

The problem with leaving it to another person (such as an adult child or other relative) is that the surviving spouse loses the benefit of the property. He or she will neither receive any income nor have the use of it since it belongs to somebody else. A solution to this, then, is to leave that amount directly to the family trust with the surviving spouse entitled to certain benefits.

The family trust

Upon the death of the first spouse, the trust will split into two sub-trusts: the family trust and the marital trust (See Exhibit 2). Some people call these "A-B" trusts, the "A" referring to the marital trust and the "B" referring to the family trust. Up to $600,000 (under current law) may pass into the family trust without adverse estate tax consequences. By doing so, not only do the heirs receive the benefit of an estate tax-savings tool, but the surviving spouse can receive the economic benefit of the funds in that trust.

The IRS allows the family trust to qualify for the first spouse's $600,000 exemption while providing funds for the surviving spouse...as long as the surviving spouse's access to this money is limited to certain "ascertainable standards," which include all of the following:

a. All the interest income from the family trust.
b. Principal as needed from the family trust for the following:

- Health
- Maintenance
- Support
- Education

c. 5 percent of the value of the family trust or $5,000 per year, whichever is greater.

By providing no more than all of the above, you can keep the value of the trust out of the estate of the surviving spouse. If the surviving spouse has access to more than the ascertainable standards, then the IRS will consider it his or her property and include it in his or her estate.

However, although there are restrictions, proper use of this trust can provide the surviving spouse with significant funds. On the other hand, the trust can be drawn to provide nothing for the surviving spouse but can, instead, provide for others, such as children.

There are several points to be aware of concerning the family trust:

- Once this trust is "funded" (after the first death), it becomes irrevocable. It cannot be changed. As such, it becomes a separate taxpaying entity that receives its own federal identification number and files its own tax return.

- A "sprinkling" provision, if properly drawn, allows the trustee to "sprinkle" or direct funds from the trust to the children. This allows him or her to provide funds to grown children without being limited by the $10,000 gift exclusion (discussed in Chapter 15).

- No matter how large the family trust becomes, the value is not subject to estate taxes when it passes to the heirs.

- While the *principal* in this trust can be free from the creditors of the surviving spouse, the *income* the spouse receives can be subject to the creditors.

- You can allow the surviving spouse a limited right to change the beneficiaries of this trust.

- Remarriage restrictions can be included in this trust by which the surviving spouse would cease to receive any funds should he or she remarry.

Marital trust

The second sub-trust is the marital trust. It consists of the surviving spouse's half of the joint trust property and, depending upon the size of your estate, it can also include the balance of the property that didn't go into the family trust. Exactly how it is structured depends upon your circumstances. Since this goes to the surviving spouse estate tax-free, it is often called the "marital deduction trust."

The major requirement, if you pass property to the surviving spouse under the unlimited marital deduction, is that, at a minimum, he or she receives the income the trust generates, paid at least annually. On the other hand, the surviving spouse may receive everything, with no limitations. And of course, it can be anything in between.

The Q-TIP trust

"Q-TIP" stands for Qualified Terminable Interest Property. This is a third sub-trust that can be used when you want the surviving spouse to have the benefit of the money but you still want to maintain some control over it. Use of this trust can still qualify for the marital deduction as long as the surviving spouse receives all the income. In addition to the income, the surviving spouse can be entitled to principal under certain conditions. Upon death of the surviving spouse, the property then passes according to the wishes of the first-to-die.

Although it might sound complicated, it really isn't. It is a way for the first-to-die to take advantage of the unlimited marital deduction by leaving property to the surviving spouse while still controlling access to that money and its ultimate destination.

There are several broad cases where this trust is used.

- A spouse wants to ensure that his/her children receive the money at the death of the surviving spouse but still allow the surviving spouse to receive income during his or her lifetime.
- The spouse wants to ensure that the funds aren't diverted to a new spouse upon remarriage.
- The spouse wants to make sure that there are controls so the money is not misused.
- A spouse wants to ensure that children from a previous marriage receive their rightful inheritance.

Let's look at two cases.

Louise and Mike Bowman (Exhibit 2) had been married 30 years when they set up their living trust. Their estate was $800,000. Mike, while concerned about saving estate taxes, wanted Louise to have access to virtually everything at his death, and vice versa. Neither was *concerned about what the other would do with the money. They were joint trustees of the living trust with the other named as successor trustee. Louise died first. The first $400,000 went into the family trust. Mike will be entitled to all the income plus principal as needed for health, maintenance, support, and education. In addition, he can receive 5 percent or $5,000 per year, whichever is greater. This trust will provide significant estate tax savings for the children upon his death. Since the Bowmans wanted the surviving spouse to receive everything else, the balance went to Mike in the marital trust with no restrictions as to its use or disposition.*

* * *

Ralph and Barbara Stone (Exhibit 3) had been married six years. Each had grown children, and each brought assets into the marriage. At the time their trust was drawn, they had a joint estate of $2 million, with each owning approximately 50 percent. Both Ralph and Barbara wanted to make sure their respective children would receive their inheritance upon the death of the second spouse. Ralph set up his trust for the first $600,000 of his property to go into the family trust. He made his wife and his bank co-trustees with income-only going to Barbara. Upon her death, the funds in that trust will go to his children. The balance of his property (assuming today's value of $400,000) will be split. $200,000 will go into the marital trust for Barbara's use. She will be the trustee with full access and control over it. Because he wanted the balance of the property to go to his children, the remaining $200,000 will go in the Q-TIP trust, with Barbara and the bank as co-trustees. Barbara will receive all the income plus principal for health needs only. At her death, the property will go to his children. Barbara's trust was set up to mirror his.

Remember Donald and Rebecca Purcell? They saddled their children with $561,180 in estate taxes. Let's see what might have been had they planned differently.

Donald Purcell was 48, his wife Rebecca was 46. They had three children, ages 21, 18 and 16. They had a total net estate of $2 million. This included the value of their home, stocks and bonds, retirement plans, personal property, his business, all life insurance and the custodial accounts they had set up for their minor children. To avoid probate and to take care of themselves in the event of a disability, they had chosen to establish a joint revocable living trust. They died within weeks of each other as the result of an automobile accident.

The first $600,000 would have gone into the family (bypass) trust with the balance going to the marital trust for the benefit of Rebecca. (If they had wished, they could have included a Q-TIP trust consisting of the balance of his property.) Upon Rebecca's death, all the money would have gone into a children's trust for the benefit of their children.

Calculating the tax

Let's calculate their estate tax had they taken advantage of a family trust (Exhibit 4).

- Mr. Purcell's share of the estate would have been the same as before, $1 million. Since he would have had a living trust, there would have been no probate expenses.
- His first $600,000 would have gone into the family trust, thereby avoiding any taxes. His remaining $400,000 balance would have gone into the marital trust and avoided taxes on that portion.
- Mrs. Purcell's adjusted gross estate would have been $1.4 million (his $400,000 balance plus her $1 million share). Remember, the $600,000 in the family trust wouldn't count against her estate.
- The gross estate tax on her $1.4 million estate would have been $512,800, less the $192,800 credit, thus resulting in a net estate tax of $320,000.
- Their children would have received $1.68 million.

As a result, the children would have received $300,780 more than they did under the previous scenario. Although the same effect could be realized if Mr. Purcell had left $600,000 directly to the children, there would be several problems. First, one of the children is a minor. We'll discuss this situation in the next chapter. Second, had Mrs. Purcell lived, she would not receive any economic benefit from that money. Third, the adult children would receive their share immediately, which might not be the Purcells' wishes. Finally, there would be no instructions at all for the use of that money.

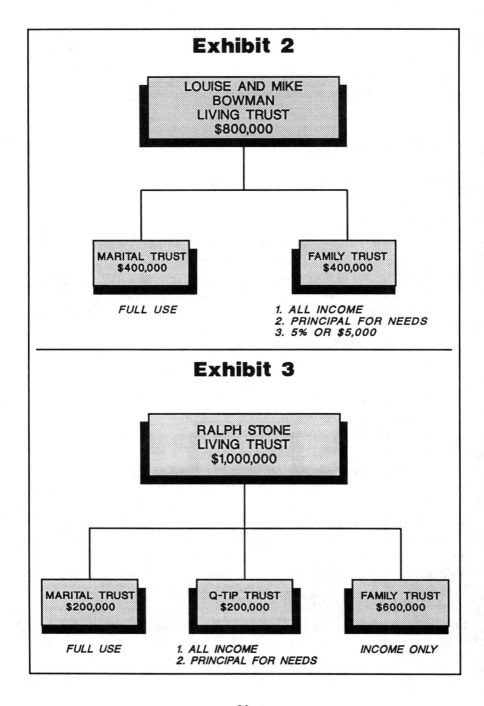

Exhibit 2

LOUISE AND MIKE
BOWMAN
LIVING TRUST
$800,000

MARITAL TRUST
$400,000

FAMILY TRUST
$400,000

FULL USE

1. ALL INCOME
2. PRINCIPAL FOR NEEDS
3. 5% OR $5,000

Exhibit 3

RALPH STONE
LIVING TRUST
$1,000,000

MARITAL TRUST
$200,000

Q-TIP TRUST
$200,000

FAMILY TRUST
$600,000

FULL USE

1. ALL INCOME
2. PRINCIPAL FOR NEEDS

INCOME ONLY

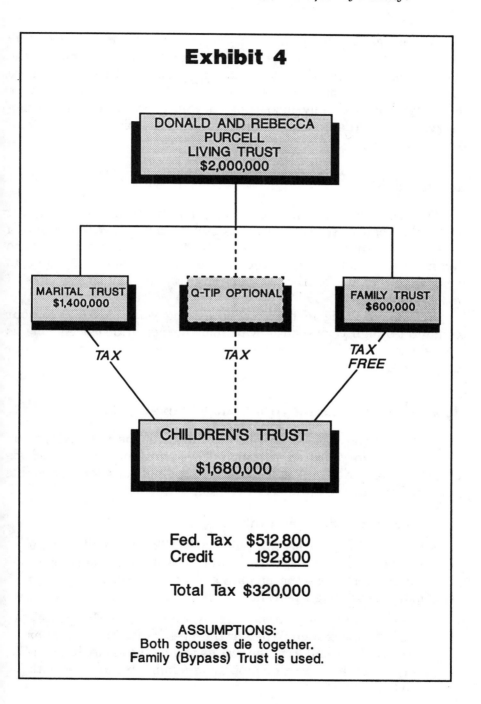

Exhibit 4

DONALD AND REBECCA PURCELL LIVING TRUST $2,000,000

MARITAL TRUST $1,400,000

Q-TIP OPTIONAL

FAMILY TRUST $600,000

TAX

TAX

TAX FREE

CHILDREN'S TRUST

$1,680,000

Fed. Tax $512,800
Credit   192,800

Total Tax $320,000

ASSUMPTIONS:
Both spouses die together.
Family (Bypass) Trust is used.

As you can see, the proper use of a trust to capture the $600,000 exemption of the first to die can save estate taxes. Although the illustrations show no estate taxes being paid at the first death, there are times when it might be wise to do so. For example, if you have property that is rapidly increasing in value, you may wish to pay estate taxes at the first death and remove that spiraling value from your estate.

Is this legal?

One question I get when discussing this estate tax savings aspect is "Is this legal?" Yes, it's legal. As stated earlier, everybody has a $600,000 exemption. You may leave $600,000 to any person estate tax-free. For example, upon your death, you can leave $600,000 to your child and the balance of your property to your spouse, free of federal estate taxes.

All we are doing in the trust is leaving your $600,000 to your children through your spouse, with some strings attached. As long as you abide by the "ascertainable standards," you can maximize your estate savings.

Tax savings by using your $600,000 exemption

The following table is provided to illustrate the tax savings you might realize in your own situation. These are only generalized examples using various taxable estates and do not consider any credits or special situations.

- Column 1 is the current value of your estate.
- Column 2 is your *net tax* (after the $192,800 credit) with a simple will (no family trust or other use of the unified credit). These figures assume probate and administrative expenses of a conservative 2 percent.
- Column 3 shows your *net tax* by capturing each spouse's $600,000 exemption. Whether this goes into a family trust or directly to the children, the results will be the same. Remember, we are assuming no probate or administration fees with the living trust.

For comparison purposes, I assumed the husband and wife died together.

Current Estate Size	Estate Taxes Without Family Trust	Estate Taxes With The Family Trust
$600,000	0	0
1,000,000	153,000	0
1,500,000	363,000	114,000
2,000,000	588,000	320,000
3,000,000	1,098,000	784,000
4,000,000	1,648,000	1,318,000
5,000,000	2,198,000	1,868,000
10,000,000	4,948,000	4,618,000

Again, you can see the significant estate tax savings by taking advantage of each spouse's $600,000 exemption.

Potential changes

I have spoken often of possible reductions in the exemption from $600,000 to as low as $200,000. While you may not have a problem today, that can change if the exemption changes. The trust will still have the same advantage. If you are married, you can take advantage of both $200,000 exemptions to give you $400,000. The concept remains the same as covered in this chapter, just the numbers are different. The end result is still significant savings.

Conclusion

As I have shown in this chapter, if you have an estate tax problem, capturing the $600,000 exemption of the first-to-die is very important. Unfortunately, it is a solution that is rarely used. That just means that Uncle Sam (and possibly your state) will get more of your estate than necessary.

While this strategy can be a big help in capturing the $600,000 exemption of both spouses, it is not the only one that can be used. In Chapter 17 we will begin looking at other techniques that can help reduce the cost of your estate taxes.

Ten

How Can I Provide for My Minor Children?

One of the saddest occurrences I see in my practice is the hardship inflicted on minor children when their parents die without the proper planning. There are too many situations where parents, either through misguided information, lack of knowledge or procrastination, structure their estates in such a manner that they totally ignore the present and future needs of their minor children.

When both parents die, the property has to go to someone. If the parents have failed to plan, then most, if not all, of their property will go to their children. Even if the parents have planned, they generally take one of two courses: 1) they leave property directly to the children; or 2) they leave it to the relative who is going to take care of the children. Let's look at each of these potentially disastrous scenarios.

Leaving property to minor children: the probate court

As you know by now, minors can't own property. So when you leave property to a minor, the probate court takes control. It appoints someone to take care of the children. Usually, this is the person named in your will, known as the *guardian*. In addition, the court will appoint a guardian of the property. In some states, this person is also called a guardian, in others a *conservator*. This person may or may not be the same as the guardian of the child. Depending on your state of residence and the circumstances, he or she may have to post a bond. Among other things, it depends on who actually received the funds: Did the children receive them directly (for example, as a beneficiary of a life insurance policy), or did they pass through the estate?

84

In the latter case, through proper planning, you probably can avoid the need for a bond.

The guardian/conservator must keep *accurate records* of how the money is used. Many states severely limit where the money can be invested and spent. If an extraordinary expense is desired (braces, etc.), then the guardian/conservator may have to go back to the court and ask permission. Often, this will require the services of an attorney, and that can get expensive. And then when the child reaches legal age, let's say 18, he or she receives the funds. What a comforting thought. My son getting all my money the day he turns 18!

How minor children end up with property

The first question is, how and why do minor children end up with property? The answers are simple: They receive it as the result of improper advice given to their parents, lack of thought or failure to properly plan. Let's explore.

A life insurance agent met with Lee Pike, who had just applied for a $500,000 policy.

Agent: *"Mr. Pike, who do you want as beneficiary?"*

Lee: *"My wife, Judith Ann Pike."*

Agent: *"If your wife doesn't survive you, who should then get the proceeds?"*

Lee: *"I guess my kids, Jeffrey, Brian and David."*

Boy, wasn't that simple? In Mr. Pike's mind, his family is totally protected. His wife will have money to care for herself and the children. If both should die, the children will have the money for their support. Perfect! Enter the dragon!

What really happened

Mr. & Mrs. Pike were on a trip to the Caribbean. They decided to take a day trip to a neighboring island aboard a small plane. A storm hit. The pilot was flying too low and crashed into the side of a mountain. Mr. and Mrs. Pike were killed.

At home, their family grieved. The children, still too young to comprehend the whole thing, were upset because their mommy and daddy weren't coming back. Luckily, Lee had taken care of his affairs. He and his wife had up-to-date wills and sufficient life insurance. Let's look at how their assets passed:

- *Home. Their home was owned jointly. Since both were dead, the home went into their estate and passed according to their wills.*
- *Investments. They had some stocks and bonds in joint accounts. Since both joint tenants were deceased, the investments passed according to their wills.*
- *Retirement benefits. Lee had a retirement plan at work. It passed according to the beneficiary designation: first to his wife, if living; otherwise, to his estate.*
- *Insurance. Lee had life insurance. We know where that went. His wife was deceased; his children got it.*

His life insurance avoided probate because it went directly to the named contingent beneficiary: his children. Everything else went through probate. Remember, the house and investments went through probate because both joint tenants were dead. The retirement plan went through probate because the contingent beneficiary was his estate.

The wills were read:

His: "I leave everything to my beloved wife, Judith Ann, if living, otherwise to my children, share and share alike."

Hers: "I leave everything to my beloved husband Lee, if living, otherwise to my children, share and share alike."

Both named her sister, Cynthia, to be guardian of the children.

That was pretty simple, wasn't it? Everything was in order, and the kids got the money. Right? Wrong! That is not the way it actually turned out.

At the time, Jeffrey was 10, Brian was 9 and David was 6. Since they were minors, they couldn't own property. What happened? The assets entered the jurisdiction of the probate court, and the dragon wasn't far behind!

Cynthia was nominated guardian of the children. Lee's brother, Alan, also wanted guardianship. Cynthia assumed that since she was named in the will, she would automatically be guardian. But remember, when you name a guardian in your will, you are only indicating your preference. It is not binding on the court.

But in this case, as usual, the judge went along with the Pikes' wishes and named Cynthia guardian of the children as well as guardian of the property (called the conservator in some states).

Without going into detail, it has turned out to be a difficult situation for all involved. Cynthia has had her hands full trying to raise her nephews along with her own children. Additionally, she has had to worry about handling her nephews' money. By the law of her jurisdiction, she has been limited as to where she can invest the money. In addition, she is required to file periodic reports with the court.

Because her house is too small for all the children (she has three of her own), everybody is constantly bickering. Ideally, she would like to add two rooms to her home or purchase another. But she can't afford it. Every time there is an extraordinary expense for the children, she has to receive the permission of the probate court. This requires the assistance of an attorney, which is running into money. The entire process is putting a lot of pressure on her, and that affects the children. Alan has offered to take two of the children off her hands, but she knows that wasn't what her sister and brother-in-law really wanted. So she continues to struggle and does the best she can. I doubt this was what Mr. and Mrs. Pike had in mind.

Mercifully, this will end someday. When Jeffrey turns 18, he will get a check for what is left from his 33 percent. When Brian turns 18 he will get a check for his 33 percent. And when David turns 18, he will receive his 33 percent. But what happens if David, due to medical, emotional or other problems, needs more money? What if medical bills are running so high that his 33 percent is eaten up? Can he get part of Jeffrey's and Brian's? No way. He is out of luck.

It is doubtful that you would deny one of your own children medical care because it would take from the others. Yet, when the probate court has control over funds for several children, it considers each child's share separate and distinct.

Why do people put their children in that situation? Two reasons: First, they don't believe they are going to die (remember the Ostrich Syndrome?). And second, they believe that even if they do die, some miracle will cause everything to work out (the Ostrich Syndrome, Part II).

When I relate a case such as the Pikes', there are those who criticize me for looking at what they think is an atypical situation. They tell me I shouldn't worry people needlessly because things usually turn out OK. I respond in two ways: First, in my experience, these situations are not that unusual. They happen every day. But second, what sense does it make to plan only for the best? That's like a physician not worrying about prescribing a certain medication because most people don't die when they take it.

Remember, *we don't think we have a problem until we have a problem.* In my opinion, *hoping for the best is malpractice.* I owe it to my clients and to you, the reader, to properly outline the problems you might be facing as a result of your current planning. Let the others try to shield their clients from potential obstacles. That is neither my style nor intent.

Leaving the money to a relative

OK. You agree that the Pikes' situation wasn't satisfactory. But you think you have the solution. Why couldn't the Pikes have left the money directly to Cynthia? That way she could have raised the kids the way she wanted, without court interference.

Just as there are potential problems when you hold property in joint tenancy with a nonspouse, there are potential problems here. They stem from the fact that as soon as Cynthia received the money, it would have been hers, not the children's. After all, she was the named beneficiary. So let's look at a few of the potential dragons.

Let's first assume the best.

> *Cynthia received the money and carefully spent it on the children as needed. She didn't waste a penny, but neither did the children have to do without. They made it through high school. She paid for their college. The day David graduated from college, she was finished with her obligation. There was money left over. So she brought*

the boys into her den, sat them down, and gave them each one-third of the money, explaining that this was what was left of the money their parents left her to take care of them.

Gift consequences. Had she done this, she would have made a *gift!* That is right. Remember, it was her money. The minute she gave it to the boys, she made what might be a taxable gift, as we will see in Chapter 15. And that is the best that could have happened. Let's look at the consequences of other scenarios.

Divorce. What would have happened had Cynthia gotten *divorced?* Whose money would it have been, anyway? It would have been hers! And her husband could have made a valid case for going after it. He could have claimed that it was part of the marital estate, accumulated during their marriage. Even if he couldn't get any of it, it could have affected the final settlement.

Lawsuit. What would have happened had Cynthia been *sued?* The money would have been her asset—all of it would have been at risk.

Death. What would have happened had Cynthia *died?* That money probably would have ended up with her husband. What if they had both died? The money would probably have gone to Cynthia's children, unless other arrangements had been made. It is doubtful that Jeffrey, Brian or David would have received anything.

All kinds of things could have happened, and they're all bad. Remember the dragons. Why take chances when there are better alternatives?

There are two things Mr. and Mrs. Pike could have done, and both involve trusts. First, they could have included a testamentary trust as part of their will. Second, they could have created a living trust. Let's look at both.

Using a trust

A *testamentary trust* is a trust created by the will. Upon the death of Mr. and Mrs. Pike, their assets would pass into the trust rather than directly to the children. They could have named Cynthia as guardian of the children and could have named Alan, or anyone else they wanted, as trustee of the property. They could have left instructions in the trust how the money was to be invested, how it was to be spent, and how it would eventually pass to the children.

While this type of trust provides definite advantages over a simple will, the problems with it are essentially the same as those of wills. First, the will must be probated. Therefore, a testamentary trust won't avoid the time delays and costs related to probate. In addition, it will be under the jurisdiction of the probate court and possibly result in some problems discussed earlier. And, of course, a contest of the will by other heirs (such as children by a previous marriage) can cause the entire will to be thrown out, and it's anyone's guess what might happen then.

If having the probate court oversee the trust is important to you, then consider the testamentary trust. If you would prefer to keep the court out of the process, then you can consider a living trust. The differences between the two trusts are covered in Chapter 12.

With a *revocable living trust*, the trust contains language that establishes a special sub-trust for your children. All your assets, if that is your desire, will flow directly into that trust. No muss, no fuss, no probate. At that point, your trustees will take over and follow your instructions.

No matter which type of trust you choose, there are some basic decisions that need to be made. Let's look at a few of them.

Guardians

One of the most difficult decisions is who will be the person or persons to rear your children? Who will be the person to give the love, affection and guidance once you are not around? This alone is the single reason that most people don't plan: They can't decide or agree on a guardian. As a result, they do nothing, and leave that decision up to the court.

The guardian should be someone who shares your values and be a person you feel would do a good job rearing your children. But realize that nobody can do as good a job as you can—nobody will care about your children as much as you do. But that is not a valid excuse for avoiding your obligation to name someone. However difficult the decision, it is still better than leaving your children's future up to the court.

The guardian is not named in the trust; he or she is named in the will. If you have a testamentary trust, then the will that contains the trust names the guardian. If you have a living trust, the documents should include a "pour-over" will, which, among other things, names a guardian for your children.

It is important to realize that your nomination of a guardian does not guarantee that choice by the court. While the court will try to honor your wishes, there may be extenuating circumstances that prevent that. For example, a natural parent will usually have the first opportunity to become the legal guardian of your common children, no matter how much you might abhor the thought.

Trustees

Once you have named someone to rear the children, you should choose a different person to take care of the financial responsibilities. That person is known as the trustee. Although the trustee and guardian can be the same person, it is preferable to have different parties occupying each position.

The trustee's first job is to handle the funds and to invest them carefully. Unlike the probate court, which in many jurisdictions allows the money to be invested only in federally insured banks, you can give the trustee as much or as little leeway as you see fit.

The second job of the trustee is to assist the guardian financially. It is the trustee who provides the guardian with the funds for your children.

What we have done is taken the two elements of rearing children, caring for them and supporting them financially, and divided them between two different parties. While parents normally handle both aspects, this is extremely difficult for a guardian who is rearing your children in addition to his or her own. It makes more sense for the guardian to care for the children and the trustee to handle the finances.

Instructions

When it comes right down to it, one of the major advantages of a trust is that it can contain your special instructions to the trustees on how to care for your loved ones. Think of your trustees as your baby sitter. Just as you leave instructions for your baby sitter when you go out for a night on the town, so you will leave instructions for your trustees in your trust.

Let's give the Pikes what they never received: a second chance. We'll see how things might have been with different planning.

Mr. and Mrs. Pike set up a revocable living trust. They titled all their property in the trust. The trust was the beneficiary of Lee's life insurance and the contingent beneficiary of his retirement plan. Upon Lee's death, the trust split into the family and marital trust. Upon Mrs. Pike's death, all the property flowed into the "children's trust." They wanted both sides of the family involved in rearing their children. In their "pour-over" will, they named Cynthia as guardian of the children. In their trust, they named Alan as trustee. Additionally, they set forth their instructions to Alan covering many different occurrences, for example:

- *The trustee was instructed to provide the necessary principal and interest for the benefit of the children.*

- *He should distribute money on the basis of need, rather than equality. For example, if David needs money for special education, it should be provided, without concern about spending an equal amount for the other children.*

- *The trustee should assist Cynthia in any manner he feels will make the environment better for the children. For example, if she needs an addition to her home and there is, in his opinion, sufficient funds without financially harming the children, then it should be done.*

- *The trustee may advance money for a business or practice when the children get older, assuming it doesn't harm the remaining children. The eventual inheritance of that child will be reduced by this amount.*

- *When the youngest child is 25 or completes college, whichever occurs first, 25 percent of the funds will be distributed equally among the boys. They will receive the remaining 75 percent in three equal installments every five years. Meanwhile, the trustee should provide funds for medical assistance should the need arise.*

- *He was instructed to hold the funds in trust should any of the boys become mentally incapacitated, using it for that child's needs for as long as he remains in that condition.*

The trust contained many more instructions for different eventualities. It was full of the Pikes' instructions for the care of their children.

Upon the deaths of their parents, the boys' futures would be assured. Cynthia, as guardian, could rear the boys to the best of her ability. Alan, as trustee, would follow all his brother's instructions. The court would not be involved. There would be no delays at all. When Cynthia needed money, she would contact Alan. Meanwhile, the money would be invested conservatively for growth. When Cynthia gets cramped in her home, there should be sufficient funds in the trust to pay for adding two bedrooms to her home. While there will be problems from time to time, there are no circumstances that Cynthia and Alan should not be able to handle. The boys would receive their inheritance when mandated by their parent's trust.

Unfortunately, in real life, this "second-chance" scenario never happened.

Conclusion

I relate the Pikes' case with the hope that their disaster will serve to show you how things can be handled with the proper planning. So many bad things can happen when dealing with minor children. Instead of releasing control of your estate to the dragons, keep it yourself. It will be much better for all involved.

Eleven

What Special Types of Trusts Are Available for Minors?

Children's trusts have the unique ability of benefiting parents (lower income and estate taxes, liability protection) while also providing advantages to their children (income, money for college, larger inheritance).

Income taxes can be reduced by shifting income to children, who are usually in lower tax brackets. Estate taxes can be reduced by gifting money now, before it appreciates. And liability can be avoided under some properly drawn children's trusts where control is out of the hands of the parents.

In recent years, the federal government has passed laws that make children's trusts less attractive. Nevertheless, there are a few trusts that can be used to your advantage.

UGMA/UGTA

Definition. UGMA, which stands for Uniform Gifts to Minors Act, allows adults to invest in certain assets as custodians for their children. The types of property invested are limited to banks, securities (stocks, bonds, mutual funds), life insurance and annuities.

UTMA, which stands for Uniform Transfer to Minors Act, is an expanded form of UGMA. Basically, it removes most of the restrictions concerning allowable investments and transfers between trusts and estates. Fewer states allow the UTMA than the UGMA.

Process. The property is held in the name of an adult, usually a parent, as custodian for the child. It reads "John Smith, Custodian for Randy Smith, under the (your state) UGMA." The property constitutes a gift to the child. Since it is a "present interest" gift, it qualifies for the $10,000 annual exclusion.

Taxes. If a parent makes the gift, serves as custodian, and dies, the property is included in his or her *estate*. However, if another party is the custodian, it is included in the estate of the child.

Income earned in the account is taxed to the minor. The party responsible for the tax depends on the age of the child.

- If the child is under the age of 14, there is no tax on the first $1,000 of investment income. Income above $1,000 is taxed to the parents at their income tax bracket.

- If the child is 14 or older, all investment income will be taxed to the child at his or her tax bracket.

Distribution of the property. The child receives the property at the age of majority, which is governed by state law. You have no choice in this matter; it is automatic by operation of law.

Advantages. Depending on the application of the tax laws explained above, it serves to get income taxed to the child instead of the parent and get assets out of the estate of the parent and into the child's, unless the parent is also the custodian. Unlike the typical trust, it is a no-cost way to put assets in the name of the child. It removes future appreciation of the assets from the estate of the parent. And trust assets can be used for health, maintenance, support and education of the child, at the custodian's discretion.

Disadvantages. The property goes to the child at the age of majority, no matter what the parent may want. The gift is also irrevocable—the parent cannot get it back if a financial emergency arises. Upon reaching the age of majority, the child may demand a formal audit of the account. The value of the account is also included in your estate if you die while acting as custodian, and your child is still a minor.

Section 2503(b) Trust

Definition. This trust, named after the IRS code section 2503(b), can provide continuous income to the child during the period he or she is a minor.

Process. A trust is established for the benefit of the child. The gifts are "present interest" gifts and qualify for the $10,000 annual exclusion. However, since the gift results in a stream of income, only the present value is included in the calculation.

Taxes. The *income* is taxable to the child under the same rules as the UGMA. If the child is under the age of 14, investment income in excess of $1,000 is taxed to parents at their tax bracket. If the child is age 14 or older, the income is taxed to the child at the child's bracket.

Distribution. While there is no requirement as to the distribution of the principal, income can last a lifetime or be directed to any person.

Advantages. The trust qualifies under the $10,000 gift exclusion and it does not require distribution of the principal to the child. The income is taxed to the child subject to above limitations. There is also a great deal of flexibility over distribution of principal.

Disadvantages. Specified income must be distributed to the child at least annually as well as all income earned. Any income not paid during the years the child was a minor must be paid out at the age of majority.

Section 2503(c) Trust

Definition. The Section 2503(c) trust allows a person to make a gift to the child but still maintain control of the property. Unlike the Section 2503(b) trust, this trust does not require mandatory distributions of income.

Process. The property is gifted into the trust for the benefit of the child. Since it is a gift of "present interest," it falls within the $10,000 annual exclusion. Income need not be paid until the child reaches age 21. At that point, the trust must be distributed to the child. However, the child can choose not to take it.

Taxes. If the donor is the trustee and dies before the child is 21, the value is included in the *estate* of the donor.

Income, if distributed, will be taxed to the child beneficiary. If the income is left to accumulate in the trust, it will be taxed to the trust itself.

Distribution. The property can be distributed to the child at age 21. However, the child can choose to leave the property in the trust while retaining the right to remove it anytime he or she desires.

Advantages. It removes the property, and the eventual appreciation, from the estate of the donor. It can also shift income from the higher bracket of the donor to the lower bracket of the child. Since the child under 14 is in the same income tax bracket as the parent (after the first $1,000 of income), this is only effective if the child is over the age of 14. The child can choose to leave property in trust beyond the age of 21. And there is no requirement for income distribution while the child is a minor.

Disadvantages. It is an irrevocable gift to the child to which the child is entitled anytime after the age of 21. The trust assets must be available to the child at age 21. Upon the death of the donor, the value of the trust is included in his or her estate if the child is under the age of 21. If the child dies before the age of 21, the trust goes to the child's estate.

Conclusion

By taking advantage of the difference in tax brackets between you and your children (and/or grandchildren), you can reduce not only your income taxes but your estate taxes as well. Combining this with sensible estate planning should be an integral part of your overall plan.

Twelve

How Do Testamentary and Living Trusts Compare?

Many attorneys criticize living trusts, claiming that they are not as valuable a planning vehicle as people are led to believe. To a point, they are correct. No matter what some people claim, living trusts are not for everyone. There are other types of planning methods that might be used, depending upon your particular situation.

However, that in no way denigrates the viability of living trusts for your planning. In fact, living trusts have some very strong arguments in their favor, as discussed earlier.

In their condemnation of living trusts, the detractors compare them with wills. And they always come up with the same few arguments: the cost of a living trust is too high; you have to transfer your property into a living trust; and probate isn't so bad. Those may or may not be valid points. But many of these same people say if you do need a trust, then you should do a testamentary trust, which is part of your will. At that point, the issue is not between a living trust and a will. It is instead between a testamentary trust containing a family trust and a living trust containing a family trust. To help clear up this conflict, it is important to look objectively at the two types of trusts.

There is a basic difference between the two trusts:

A **testamentary** trust is part of your will and takes effect at your death.

A **living** trust is in force during your lifetime *and* after your death.

The issues

Cost. The cost of a testamentary trust will fall somewhere between a will and a living trust. As a result, a testamentary trust should initially cost less than a living trust. Consider, however, that the testamentary trust must be probated. Therefore, no matter how easy probate may be, the total cost for a testamentary trust should be greater than that of the living trust.

There are some who say that for the attorney, the testamentary trust is the best of all worlds: Not only can he charge more for drafting a will containing a testamentary trust, he also gets to probate the will. In some businesses, that would be considered "double-dipping." Personally, when I was faced with the choice between a testamentary trust and a living trust, I chose to spend a little more initially for a living trust. That way, I could enjoy the living benefits of the trust and keep my family out of probate.

One last point concerning cost. Considering inflation, the cost of probate most certainly will go up. If you do a living trust now, you have frozen your cost at the price of the trust today.

Probate. As long as your property is titled in your revocable trust, it avoids probate. A testamentary trust, being part of a will, guarantees probate and all its problems.

Disability. Your revocable trust contains your instructions for taking care of you and your family in the event of mental incapacity. A testamentary trust doesn't take effect until your death, and therefore does nothing for disability planning.

Save estate taxes. Both a living trust and a testamentary trust can save estate taxes for married couples.

Contestation. While it is extremely difficult to successfully contest a living trust, it is easy to contest a will containing a trust.

Ongoing fees during life. Since a testamentary trust is not valid during life, no ongoing fees are required. Neither are any ongoing fees required, under normal circumstances, with a living trust.

Tax forms. Neither trust requires any special tax forms until after the death of the first spouse. No special forms are required during life.

Transferring property. For a living trust to avoid probate, the trustmaker must transfer his property to the trust before his death. Nothing is transferred into a testamentary trust until death. But if you think that it is hard for you to transfer your property into the trust *now*, think about what your family will have to go through when you're not around!

Problems with testamentary trusts

There is one vital point that most people seem to ignore when they tout testamentary trusts: *Most of the property of the first-to-die normally bypasses the will and never makes it into the testamentary trust in the first place.* Most couples own the bulk of their assets jointly. That means that if you don't change the title of your property out of joint ownership (and most people don't), the testamentary trust is totally worthless. That's because jointly owned property bypasses the will and goes directly to the surviving tenant. As a result, the testamentary trust holds virtually no property, totally defeating its purpose.

Ann and Chris Tanner's estate was valued at $1.5 million. Their planner suggested setting up a testamentary trust to save estate taxes. They met with their attorney, and he drafted the trust. They went home thinking they would save a significant amount of taxes. Their property was owned as follows:

Home	*Jointly owned*	*$500,000*
Brokerage Account	*In Chris's name*	*$100,000*
Retirement Plan	*Payable to Ann*	*$550,000*
Life Insurance	*Payable to Ann*	*$200,000*
Bank Account #1	*In Ann's name*	*$125,000*
Bank Account #2	*In Chris's name*	*$25,000*

Chris died. Unfortunately, things didn't quite work out the way they had planned. In spite of the fact that they had a testamentary trust, not much of the property actually made it into the trust, as the following reveals.

Home	Directly to Ann	
Brokerage Account	**Into the trust**	**$100,000**
Retirement Plan	Directly to Ann	
Life Insurance	Directly to Ann	
Bank Account #1	Stayed in Ann's name	
Bank Account #2	**Into the trust**	**$25,000**

Of all their property, only the brokerage account ($100,000) and Chris' bank account ($25,000) went into the family trust. The rest of the assets went directly to Ann by operation of law. The result was that instead of taking advantage of the $600,000 exemption upon Chris' death by passing that much into a family trust, only $125,000 passed into the trust. This may end up costing them potentially hundreds of thousands of dollars in estate taxes.

No good solutions

As you can see, they received little value from the testamentary trust. What could they have done to make the testamentary trust more valuable?

Let's look first at what Chris could have done.

He could have changed the beneficiary on his life insurance from Ann to the trust. That would have increased the amount flowing into the family trust from $125,000 to $325,000. But that still would have been well short of the $600,000 he would have needed to receive maximum benefit.

He could have changed the beneficiary designation on his retirement plan from Ann to the trust. The problem with doing that is a rule that affects retirement accounts: If the surviving spouse receives the benefits upon the death of the account holder, he or she can roll it into an IRA and defer the income taxes until he or she starts making withdrawals. If anybody else (such as a trust) receives those benefits, it is subject to income taxes immediately. In this case, although the $550,000 could have gone into the family trust, doing so would have made the entire amount immediately subject to income taxes. (We're not going to even discuss the effect of the "success tax" covered in Chapter 20.)

The only remaining viable alternative would have been to change the ownership on their home from "Joint Tenants With Rights of Survivorship" to "Tenants in Common." That would effectively split the ownership of the home in two, allowing Chris' half to flow into the family trust upon his death. Beside the fact that he would still be short of the $600,000, his half of the house would have had to go through probate. It is bad enough that jointly owned property must go through probate at the second death. Not too many people are excited about the idea of taking property that would have been probate-free at the first death and forcing it through probate.

And what if Ann had died first? Let's look at the alternatives.

The only thing that would have helped in the event that Ann died first would have been to change the ownership of the home as discussed earlier. Even then, only $400,000 ($275,000 from half the house and the $125,000 bank account) would have gone into the family trust. This would have left her still short of the optimum $600,000. The only way she would have had enough property to hit the $600,000 figure would have been to put the home totally in her name. But that would have put Chris well short of the $600,000. And again, potentially probate-free property would have been forced through the probate process.

A joint living trust, on the other hand, would have allowed the first $600,000 to go into the family trust, no matter which spouse died first. They could have taken advantage of the $600,000 exemption and avoided probate. To me, it makes no sense to force property through probate when that can easily be avoided with a living trust.

What's the justification?

As I review the problems Ann and Chris faced, I have a real problem with attorneys who recommend testamentary trusts over living trusts. You can see the two main problems that are created. First, you have to change jointly owned property into individually owned or tenants in common. Second, you must make your life insurance benefits payable to your estate. In both cases, property that would ordinarily pass probate free must be forced through probate.

Does that make sense to you? Can you see any justification for doing this? Even if probate is no problem, as some attorneys contend, you still have the other advantages inherent in a living trust.

In my opinion, forcing property through probate is like a CPA making a mistake on your tax return just to force you through an audit. It's like a surgeon leaving a scalpel in the patient during an operation just so he can charge for another operation. There is just no justification.

Equalization

One other factor that needs to be considered in structuring estates has to do with a concept known as "equalization."

Robert and Michelle McMahon's estate was valued at $2.4 million, the bulk of which consisted of a home ($500,000), his business ($1.2 million) and his life insurance ($400,000). The balance of the property consisted of bank accounts and personal belongings. The home, business and insurance were owned by Robert. The balance was equally owned. The problem was that if Michelle were to die first, only $150,000 (half the other property) would be available to take advantage of the $600,000 exemption. This could result in unnecessary estate taxes at Robert's death.

It was recommended that the McMahons "equalize" their estates by putting sufficient property into Michelle's name to bring her up to $600,000. This could have been done one of three ways: retitling the home in Michelle's name; splitting ownership of the business between Robert and Michelle; or placing their assets in a joint living trust.

The attorney recommended the living trust because it would allow Bob to maintain partial control over all the assets while saving probate costs and estate taxes. Although there were other methods that could have been used, the attorney felt this was the best.

Conclusion

Let's compare a testamentary trust and a living trust using our definition of estate planning.

"During my life and after my death, I want to control and distribute my property in the manner I desire, minimizing all fees, taxes and court interference, preserving for myself, my family, and those I choose, the estate I have worked so hard to create."

	Testamentary trust	Living trust
Effective during your life	No	Yes
Effective after your death	Yes	Yes
Control property as you desire	Yes	Yes
Distribute it as you desire	Yes	Yes
Minimize fees (other than set-up)	No	Yes
Minimize taxes	Yes	Yes
Minimize court interference	No	Yes

To review, a living trust can do all that a testamentary trust can do, but the reverse isn't necessarily true. A testamentary trust has limits. And back to my old argument: If you are going to spend additional money to have a trust drawn, why not consider a living trust, which will avoid probate and a possible contest, keep your affairs private, cost less in the long run, hold all your property, care for your family following your death *and* care for you upon your disability?

Thirteen

How Do I Know if I Need a Living Trust?

To this point, we have discussed a variety of planning issues, with more to come. Much of our discussion has revolved around, and will continue to revolve around, revocable living trusts. Nevertheless, there is still the determination of whether a living trust is for you. To help sort out the issues, let's review some areas where it might be helpful.

Which is better for you...a trust or a will?

First, understand that I make no money from wills or trusts. I am unbiased, with no ax to grind other than to help you make the best decisions *for you*. Though I prefer a living trust for my own situation, it's not for everybody. So let's look at some questions you need to consider.

Are you married with an estate larger than $600,000?

If the answer to this question is "yes," you have an estate tax problem. You learned from our earlier discussion that each person can pass the equivalent of $600,000 upon his or her death. Anything greater than that is subject to estate taxes. If you wish to reduce your estate taxes, you will want to capture the $600,000 exemption of each spouse. Remember, under traditional planning, the exemption of the first-to-die is usually lost. So let's again review the ways to capture it.

- Leave the property outright to a person other than your spouse. Doing this has its own disadvantages. Mainly, the property would be gone, and the surviving spouse would receive no further benefit from it. But if the surviving spouse does not need that money, then this is an option.

- Give it away. During your life you may gift money as you want. Any gifts over your annual $10,000 exclusion will count against your $600,000 lifetime exemption, as discussed in Chapter 15.

- Use a trust. If you want to keep control of the property, if you don't want to give it away during your life, and if the surviving spouse needs the income from the property, then a trust is undoubtedly the best alternative. You know by now that my preference in this case would be a living trust rather than a testamentary trust.

Do you have minor children?

If you do, the only decision you need to make is whether you want to write the rules for their care, or you want the court to write the rules. If it is the former, then, in my opinion, the most effective way to care for your children is through a trust. You name a guardian for the children in your will; you name trustees for the property in your trust. In addition, you can specify how you want them cared for and when they should receive their inheritance. Again, the choice is between a living trust and a testamentary trust.

Do you wish to avoid probate?

Although probate may not be as bad as some people make it out to be, it is an issue that must be considered. Your state laws, the composition of your assets, and the way your assets are owned are but a few factors that affect the probate process. You might feel more comfortable under the supervision of the probate court. And while it might be advantageous to go through probate, those situations are rare. Remember, property titled in a living trust avoids probate. While that alone may not be the only reason to do a living trust, it is important.

Are you concerned about your mental disability?

If you're not, you should be. We never know when we are going to become incapable of handling our own financial affairs. There are

106

really only two ways to resolve this. One way is a power of attorney, which is discussed in Chapter 23. The other way is through a living trust, which names successor trustees and contains instructions in case of your disability. Remember, a testamentary trust (part of a will) is of no benefit during a disability.

Are you concerned about a contest of your estate?

As discussed earlier, the probate court is a forum for contesting a will. While a living trust doesn't guarantee protection, contesting it is much more difficult.

Do you own property in different states?

Wills are interpreted under different rules in different states. In addition, if you own property in other states, you must go through probate in each of those locales. A living trust avoids this.

Are you married and wish to protect assets?

Many professionals and business people face liability threats. Normally, they place their assets in the name of the nonexposed spouse. Chapter 27 covers a way you can use a living trust to protect your assets. While living trusts are not designed to be a protection mechanism, they can be useful in this area.

Are a spouse's financial skills a concern?

In many marriages, one person totally handles the financial affairs. In these cases, the surviving spouse is often left with substantial funds but no training in managing them. With a living trust, you can name trustees or co-trustees to make sure your spouse is cared for and the money is not wasted.

Do you want to guarantee your children's inheritance?

Many people are concerned about what will happen to their assets upon their deaths. They are especially concerned if they have children. How can they be sure the children will, in fact, end up with the money? What happens if the surviving spouse remarries and loses that money to his or her new spouse? A properly drawn trust can take care of this potential problem.

Are you concerned about the initial cost?

Probably, the answer is "yes." But before making up your mind, let me ask you a few questions. Are the points made previously of concern to you? If so, do you think the living trust can solve them? If the answers to these questions are yes, then the living trust could prove advantageous to you.

If you are concerned about the cost, let me ask you one more question. *If a living trust were to cost the same as a will, which would you choose?* If your answer is a living trust, then the question is not between the will and the trust. Rather, it is whether it is worth the extra initial cost to do a trust. That is a decision only you can make.

Living trusts vs. wills

In the previous chapters, we discussed the differences between living trusts, testamentary trusts and simple wills. I pointed out my preference for living trusts because of the many advantages I believe they offer.

Understand the major difference between a will and a trust: A simple will is a simple document in which you specify how you want your property to pass upon your death. A living trust is a document that becomes effective immediately and can solve many planning problems that we discussed. Most people with whom I speak agree that a living trust, moreso than a will, fulfills our definition of estate planning.

If that is true, if the living trust has all these advantages, why is there so much controversy? Why are so many attorneys against the living trust? Why do they continue to favor wills?

There are several possible answers: tradition, honest belief, ignorance or money. Either they feel comfortable with wills because that is what they know, or they honestly doubt that the probate system is so bad, or they haven't been adequately trained in trusts, or they like the money they make from probate. In any case, it is a situation not likely to change.

It is the Hatfields and the McCoys...the Democrats and the Republicans...the Giants and the Dodgers. It will never be resolved to everyone's satisfaction. There will always be two sides, each disagreeing with the other.

So now it's up to you to decide. After all, it has been the public who has picked up the living trust ball and decided to run with it. If we, as Americans, didn't see probate as a problem, we wouldn't be concerned. If we hadn't experienced delays, we wouldn't care. If it didn't cost us money, we wouldn't be upset. But we are. Unfortunately, most attorneys have yet to accept this.

Greyhound vs. Delta

I liken this controversy to transportation. If you have to get from Denver to Dallas, you have several choices. Among them, you can go by bus or plane. To me, the bus is like traditional will planning. The plane is like the modern living trust planning. Both will eventually get you where you want to go. The bus will be cheaper initially. But if you are in business, you might lose time, which translates into money. The bus ride might be slower. It will have many stops, delays and turns. You might get tired, bored or upset. But you will get there. The plane will cost more initially. However, the ride will be smoother, much more pleasant and save considerable time.

Now, if you talk to the bus driver, he doesn't think anything is wrong with traveling by bus. In fact, he thinks it is enjoyable. He figures "What's the rush?" As they say, relax and enjoy the ride. And if someone asks him about flying, he will try to talk him or her into taking the bus. Besides, he isn't qualified to pilot a plane. His job is at stake.

The Delta pilot can't understand that. While he could probably drive a bus, he can't understand why everyone doesn't want to fly and arrive at their destination more efficiently and pleasantly.

This may be a little farfetched, but to me it is a good analogy. Trusts are the modern way to plan. They are more expensive initially, but probably less expensive in the long run. Yet, to try to get one side to agree that the other is better is impossible. And that is our problem. We are face to face, guns drawn, neither side willing to flinch. It becomes necessary for you to decide for yourself.

Earlier I said that one of the more difficult problems working with living trusts is the number of advisors and attorneys who are not willing to accept the merits. This is especially true when living trusts are first introduced into a community. Nevertheless, I am truly amazed, when addressing groups of people from across the country, by the number of people who have living trusts. This shows the national level of acceptance, no matter what local detractors may say.

Things to watch out for

As you entertain the use of a living trust, here are some factors with which to concern yourself.

1. Make sure the attorney is knowledgeable. Estate planning is a very specialized area. Only a relatively small number of attorneys are properly trained in this field. Make sure that the attorney you choose knows what he or she is doing. Interview more than one, if necessary. Talk to friends and various professionals. If the attorney isn't familiar with this type of planning, move on to another one. Keep searching until you can find one who will do what you want. Remember, this is your plan.

2. Beware of "do-it-yourself" books. There are many people who try to save money by buying a book of forms (or computer software) with which to do their own living trust. They skim through to find the forms they think apply to their situation, and complete them. Who knows what will happen from that point forward? Those forms may or may not work. Most of them are difficult to understand. They may not be valid in your state. They may not fit your needs. Why spend a lifetime accumulating an estate and then destroy it because you want to save a few bucks? If you are going to do it at all, do it right. Work with an experienced estate planning attorney. It will be money well spent.

3. Watch out for the living trust "businesses." These are the folks "selling" living trusts. They are not attorneys. They are just ordinary folks holding seminars and using other methods to get you to buy a living trust. Possibly, they will have you complete a set of forms and mail it to an attorney somewhere to do the legal work. You may never meet face to face with an attorney. Or you might not meet with the attorney until he or she delivers the trust. Possibly they will supply you with a completed trust and suggest that you take it and review it with your own attorney. You may be asked to write two checks: one to the attorney and one to the living trust salesperson. In any case, I am concerned. You need to talk with a knowledgeable attorney *before* taking any action. You are paying for an attorney—you deserve to have his or her advice before proceeding. You deserve the best. Again, don't try to short cut.

Conclusion

Estate planning is serious business. You need an unbiased opinion as to the best course for you. Obviously, this is difficult because everyone seems to have an ax to grind. That is why I am presenting all sides in this book and letting you see for yourself the advantages and disadvantages of various planning methods. Once you decide to take action, please work with a professional. It's one thing to buy a book on how to fix a leaky faucet. It's another thing to fix your own leaky estate. Leave it to a professional.

Fourteen

How Do I Live With My Living Trust?

If you and your attorney have decided that a living trust is for you, then you will do things a little differently than you have in the past. Let's go through some of those changes, starting with the way your property is titled.

Titling your trust

Like a corporation, a trust has its own name. The title of your trust includes these important elements: trustees, trustmakers and trust date. Earlier, we saw how Mr. and Mrs. Jones titled their trust:

"Robert C. Jones and Mary F. Jones, trustees, or their successors in trust, under the Robert C. and Mary F. Jones Living Trust, dated Feb. 4, 1994, and any amendments thereto."

Your documents

1. The living trust. Obviously, the centerpiece of your planning will be the trust itself. As we have discussed, this will be where you name your trustees and beneficiaries and include your instructions for the care of those beneficiaries.

2. Pour-over will. The Joneses' living trust should also include a separate "pour-over" will, which does two things:

1. It names a guardian for their minor children.

2. It puts (pours-over) into the trust any property that is not in the trust at their deaths.

This last point is very important. Ideally, the Joneses' property will be titled in the name of their trust. However, it is possible that, for one reason or another, some of their property might still be titled in their names when they die. If that happens, that property will pass according to their will, not according to their trust.

With a pour-over will, any property not titled in the Joneses' trust at their death will automatically go (pour over) into the trust and follow the instructions contained therein. Although this property will go through probate, it will at least get into the trust.

3. Affidavit of trust. One of the cumbersome aspects of a living trust is proving to various institutions that you are, in fact, a trustee of a legitimate trust. One way to do this is to carry the trust with you and show it to the institutions. However, one of the advantages of a trust is that it is a private document, and there is no reason to carry it around and show it to everyone. One way to avoid this, and ensure your privacy, is with an affidavit of trust.

The affidavit of trust is a notarized form that indicates: 1) the legal name of the trust; 2) the title of the trust; and 3) the current trustee(s). This form, when attached to the sections of the trust that are important to the financial institution (the title page, statement of revocability, successor trustees, the powers, the signature pages, etc.), will give them the information they need and eliminate the need to provide the entire document.

Transferring property into the trust

Your trust need not include a list of your assets, any more than IBM's corporate charter lists the property it owns. Instead, title your assets in the name of the trust, thereby indicating ownership.

Once your attorney has drafted your living trust, the first thing you need to do is transfer your property into the trust. Remember, you don't *have to* transfer all your property into the trust, but whatever you don't transfer must go through probate.

One problem we face is that many attorneys and planners are interested in nothing more than selling living trusts. But drafting the trust is just part of the process—the property needs to be transferred into the trust as well, otherwise many advantages of the trust are lost. Although many critics of trusts consider transferring property a problem, in my experience, it isn't.

As a matter of practice, my firm helps our trust clients transfer their property. Once the attorney has completed the trust documents, he or she prepares new deeds for the real estate. My assistants then help our clients transfer all their other assets by preparing the necessary letters and paperwork. At this point let's look at the various types of property and how the transfer can be accomplished.

1. Real estate. You indicate ownership of real estate by a deed. That deed contains the name of the owner. Therefore, to transfer the ownership of real estate from yourself to the trust, you need a new deed. This is usually done by an attorney, although you can do it yourself. Normally, a new warranty deed is prepared under which the old owners (you and your spouse) convey the property to the new "owners," your living trust. In the Joneses' case above, the new owners of the property will be:

"Robert C. Jones and Mary F. Jones, trustees, or their successors in trust, under the Robert C. and Mary F. Jones Living Trust, dated Feb. 4, 1994, and any amendments thereto."

Because you are transferring your property from yourself to yourself, this transfer does not activate the "due on sale" clause of a mortgage. You are not changing the terms of the mortgage. You are still responsible for it. You can still qualify for the homestead exemption. You are just changing the title of the property being held as collateral.

2. Bank accounts. How you change the name on your bank accounts depends on the type of account.

You can change your *checking account* by changing the name on the bank's records. Even with computerization, most banks still use a card that shows the name on the account and contains your signatures. Most banks that I have worked with don't require that the trust name be reflected on the checks themselves. You can imagine the confusion of a cashier at your local supermarket if you present a check drawn on a trust account.

You can change the name on your *savings account* by informing the bank that you wish to change the account into your trust.

Some banks allow you to change the name on your *certificates of deposit* without penalty. Other banks want to charge you a penalty, as if you are redeeming it prematurely. If this occurs, you might want to wait until renewal to make the change, or threaten to change banks.

Your bank will want proof that the trust exists, the names of the trustees and the powers of the trustees. The affidavit of trust should handle this. Otherwise, just take the trust to the bank and let them make copies of the sections they need.

3. Automobiles, boats, campers, etc. This is one area where you run into differing state laws. In some states, you need to transfer the titles into the name of the trust if you wish to avoid probate. In some states, these items can be transferred after death without probate. In some states, there might be a transfer tax required. Check with your local authorities to learn your state's rules.

4. Brokerage accounts. While the title of bank accounts can usually be changed, that is not the case with brokerage accounts. Once an account has been established, the name on that account cannot be changed. Instead, an entirely new account with a new number is established. Then the assets are transferred from the old account to the new one.

The new account should be titled in the name of the trust. The old account owners (again, presumably you and/or your spouse), will provide a letter of authorization to the brokerage firm to transfer the assets from your old account into the trust account.

As with the bank, the affidavit of trust with the applicable powers is all they need. They do not need the entire trust—and don't give it to them.

5. Mutual funds. Although each mutual fund has its own procedures, they are pretty standardized. They require a letter from the old account holder (you and/or your spouse) instructing the fund to change the name of the account to the trust name. You must get your signature *guaranteed* (not notarized) by a bank or brokerage firm.

6. Stocks and bonds. If you have the stock and bond certificates yourself (as opposed to having them held in a brokerage account), then you should send a letter to each transfer agent along with the old certificate containing the instructions on how you want the certificate re-registered. Again, you must get your signature guaranteed. Be sure you make the certificates "non-negotiable" (a broker can tell you how), and send the certificates "registered mail—return receipt requested."

7. Life insurance. This one is easy. The owner of the policy writes a letter to the insurance company instructing it to change the beneficiary to the name of the trust. Some companies require that you use their own forms. In that case, they will mail them to you.

Since life insurance goes to a named beneficiary, or named contingent beneficiary, thus avoiding probate, some people question the necessity for making any changes, especially if there are no minors involved. But there are several reasons for doing this.

First, if you are married and have an estate tax problem, you will want to get money into the family trust. If the proceeds pass directly to the spouse, this won't happen.

Second, if you are concerned about how the money will be used if it goes directly to a beneficiary, the trust can contain your instructions and limitations.

Third, if one of the beneficiaries is disabled and not able to handle his or her own affairs, then having the proceeds payable to the trust can avoid the "living probate" problems discussed in Chapter 23.

Fourth, if one of the beneficiaries or contingent beneficiaries is deceased, the trust will indicate the ultimate distribution of the funds.

Finally, if all of the primary and contingent beneficiaries are deceased, it will keep the proceeds out of your estate, thus avoiding probate.

8. Retirement accounts. This is the trickiest area of all because of the unique rules involving retirement plans.

Barry McLean works for a major corporation. He has been contributing to a 401k for the past 10 years. In addition, he has some IRAs that he started in the early 1980s. The beneficiary on all these accounts is his wife, Marie; the contingent beneficiaries are his adult children, equally.

Here is the problem. With retirement accounts, if the beneficiary is a spouse, he or she can roll them into an IRA (regardless of the amount) without any income taxes due. There will be income taxes, however, on any amount the spouse eventually receives from the roll-over account. On the other hand, if the benefits are received by any-one other than the spouse, the entire benefit is subject to current income taxes. So if you make the living trust the beneficiary of a retirement account, the benefits become income taxable to the trust, even if the beneficiary of the living trust is the spouse.

Therefore, we usually leave the spouse as primary beneficiary of the retirement account, but make the trust the contingent (secondary) beneficiary. In the above case, if Marie is alive when Barry dies, she can receive the benefits and roll them into an IRA herself. She can then make the trust the beneficiary of her rollover account. If she is not alive when Barry dies, then the trust will receive the benefits, and they will be distributed according to its instructions. As another alternative, she can disclaim the asset, and it will go into the trust.

If you are not married, then you can just change the primary beneficiary to the trust. In either case, make sure you check with your professional advisors to determine the best way to handle it.

9. Tax-deferred annuity. A tax-deferred annuity works similarly to the IRA. If the spouse receives the benefits, that money is not income taxable to him or her until the interest is withdrawn. However, if those benefits are received by anybody other than the surviving spouse, the growth in the account is subject to income taxes.

Therefore, if you are married, make your surviving spouse the beneficiary of the annuity and the trust the contingent beneficiary. If you are not married, make the living trust the primary beneficiary.

10. Savings bonds. Department of the Treasury Form PD 1851 is used to change the registration on savings bonds from your name to your trust. The form states that you do not have to report any deferred income at that time as long as you meet the "grantor trust provisions of the Internal Revenue Code and you are treated as the owner of that portion of the trust represented by any tax-deferred accumulated interest on the reissued bonds."

11. Untitled property. What about your personal effects: jewelry, household goods, etc.? Those items aren't titled. How are they handled? One of two ways.

117

1. Your trust can state that all other property will be considered part of the trust and will pass according to the instructions contained therein.
2. Many trusts will provide a separate mechanism for transferring special items. For example, you want your wedding ring to go to your daughter, your gun collection to your son, and your coin collection to your granddaughter.

Buying and selling property

Many people question the difficulty of buying and selling property in the trust. Actually, it's quite simple. When you buy a piece of real estate, you merely instruct the closing attorney to title it in the name of the trust. When you sell property owned by the trust, you merely sell it as trustee of the trust. Nothing has to be done with the trust. Remember, the trust doesn't list your property. Ownership is indicated by the title.

Special bequests

A trust, like a will, allows you to provide special bequests for those you wish to remember. The best way to do this, other than the untitled property discussed previously, is to indicate in your trust the person(s) to whom you want the property to pass. This might be a specific amount of money you want to leave to a certain party. It might be a certain piece of property. You can handle it however you desire. On the other hand, instead of tying your trustee's hands by assigning certain property to each beneficiary, you might find it easier to specify the percentage to each, and let the trustees divide it to the mutual benefit of everyone involved.

One other point concerning percentages and dollar figures: There is a tendency to specify dollar figures when leaving money to beneficiaries who are not your children—grandchildren, for example, or nieces, nephews, charities, etc. The problem with doing that is: 1) inflation might make the dollars worth a mere fraction of what you thought; or 2) your estate might dwindle due to unforeseen circumstances, and the amount they end up receiving could be a larger percentage than you had intended. Therefore, many people choose instead to use percentages to keep all the numbers relative.

Where to keep your trust

The question always arises about where the trust should be kept: in the home or in a safe deposit box. I recommend that the attorney draft and execute two sets of the trust. The original can be kept at home and the duplicate original given to a relative, successor trustee, or put in the box at the bank.

The problem of keeping your only copy at the bank is that if the safe deposit box is sealed at your death, it will be difficult for your successor trustee to get in. The problem with keeping the only copy at home is, in case of a fire, it could be destroyed. With two original sets, you are better protected.

In addition, your trust is a "living" document. You will want to refer to it. You will want to ensure that it constantly meets your desires. Keeping it handy makes that easier.

Special instructions

You should also leave instructions about the following:

- Special instructions for burial.
- A list of your key advisors (attorney, accountant, etc.).
- Location list of your important papers.
- A list of benefits to which you may be entitled.
- Any anatomical gift instructions.
- Safe deposit box instructions.

You can see the importance of letting people know any special instructions and locations of key items. This is true whether or not you have a trust. These items are important and can make the task of those you leave behind easier.

These instructions should be included with your living trust documents. While not part of the trust, file them together so your successor trustees can find them. While most of the above are pretty simple, anatomical gift instructions must follow your state's laws.

Asset list

It is important that you leave a complete list of your assets and the location of specific documents. You probably have bank accounts at different institutions. You may have several brokerage accounts. You probably have many different insurance policies. Many heirs come across certificates or insurance policies from their parents' estates. They have no idea if the policies have any value. They may have been policies that were canceled years ago. There may be stock certificates that became worthless in 1962. They just don't know. That causes a lot of grief, because it isn't easy to track those things down.

As with the special instructions discussed previously, providing your heirs with a complete list of what you have and letting them know where it is can make settling your estate so much easier. Believe me, they will appreciate your efforts.

Caution

I have said this before, and I'll say it again. One of the disadvantages in buying a book that just has living trust forms is that you don't get proper advice. You don't know the proper way to set up your trust. You don't know what provisions to include. And you don't know what to do when the trust is finally established. I don't believe that these important decisions should be left to chance and inexperience. Please, consult a professional and make sure everything is handled properly.

Conclusion

Although what we have discussed in this chapter might sound complicated, it really isn't. Hopefully, those who have helped you with the trust will assist you in this process. The job of planning isn't worth starting if it is not properly completed. Make sure you obtain proper assistance and advice in transferring your assets.

Part III

Reducing Your Estate Taxes

Fifteen

How Can Gifting Reduce Estate Taxes?

One of the estate-reduction techniques I usually recommend when working with large estates is a planned gifting program. It is important to familiarize yourself with the rules because gifting affects so many different areas of estate planning. Earlier chapters covered transferring property into joint tenancy, giving assets to children, and calculating estate taxes, all of which have gift-tax implications. Future chapters examine removing life insurance from your estate and other advanced techniques, many of which involve gifting.

Proper use of gifting is ignored by most people. The reason for this is a lack of understanding of its advantages and uses. Additionally, there is a lot of misunderstanding concerning this area due to the number of law changes over the years.

The definition of a gift

While you and I know what we consider to be a gift, all that really matters is the Internal Revenue Service's definition. It is relatively simple: *Anytime you transfer property to another party for less than its fair market value, you have made a gift.*

The rules

- Each year, you may gift $10,000 (in cash or property) to each person you wish, free of gift taxes.
- You may transfer to your spouse unlimited amounts of cash or property with no gift tax implications.

- If you are married, you and your spouse may agree to make a joint gift (called "gift splitting") of $20,000 free of gift taxes, to each person you want in any year. Even if you make that gift with your money, it will be considered a joint gift if your spouse consents.
- If you make a gift over $10,000, or you and your spouse make a split gift (as defined previously), you are required to file a gift tax return.
- If the gift results in a tax obligation (as discussed below), the giver, not the receiver, is responsible for any gift taxes.
- There are no income taxes due either in giving or receiving a gift.
- To qualify under the annual exclusion, the gift must be a "present interest." That means that the recipient must have full and immediate access and use of the property. You cannot make a gift with "strings attached." For example, if you give your son 100 shares of IBM but say, "You can't sell this for five years," it won't qualify under the annual exclusion.
- There are no gift tax implications if you pay another person's medical costs or education expenses. As long as you actually pay the bill, as opposed to giving that person the money and letting him or her pay, you don't have to worry about gift taxes. Additionally, there is no dollar limit on the money that can be spent, and no restriction on whom that person can be.
- Any amount you gift over $10,000 effectively reduces your $600,000 combined gift and estate credit equivalent, which we have been referring to as your $600,000 exemption.
- If you guarantee a loan for another person, that guarantee is considered a gift at the time you make it, even if it is never needed.

Unified gift and estate tax

Our tax code provides for a unified gift and estate tax calculation. You remember from previous discussions that upon your death, you can pass an unlimited amount of property to your spouse, estate tax-free and can pass the equivalent of $600,000 to other persons as a group. Upon your spouse's death, he or she can pass another $600,000 free of estate taxes.

If, during your lifetime, you make a gift over $10,000, then you must file a gift tax return, and the amount of the gift over $10,000 reduces your $600,000 exemption. Remember, you really have a $192,800 tax credit, but for illustrative purposes, we use the value of that credit, $600,000.

> *In 1990, Ralph and Martha Jenkins gave their daughter $20,000. They agreed to make it a joint gift and thus were required to file a gift tax return. However, since it fell within the exclusion ($10,000 each), there was no gift tax due.*
>
> *In 1991, Mr. and Mrs. Jenkins gifted another $60,000 to their daughter. Again, they make 'it a joint gift, effectively meaning that each made a gift of $30,000. But this time there was an additional factor: what to do about the $40,000 overage? Since they each were considered to have made a gift of $30,000, they each exceeded their $10,000 exclusion by $20,000. As a result, they filed a gift tax return, and had to reduce each of their $600,000 exemptions by $20,000, making it $580,000. Upon Mr. and Mrs. Jenkins' death, they can pass only $580,000 estate tax free instead of $600,000.*

There are, of course, ways to take maximum advantage of gifting. For example, had Mr. and Mrs. Jenkins each made a gift to their daughter and son-in-law, they could have made joint gifts totaling $40,000 before encroaching into their lifetime maximum of $600,000. They could have also made gifts to each of their grandchildren, although, as discussed previously, there are special considerations with minor children.

Estate under $600,000

If your estate isn't valued at more than $600,000, and you haven't used any of your $600,000 exemption, then the amount of a gift will have no affect at all.

> *Mr. Jenkins' mother was elderly and could no longer live alone. Mr. Jenkins decided to have her move in with them. She had an estate of $250,000. After she moved in, she decided to sign everything over to him. Her gift was $240,000 after subtracting her $10,000 exclusion, resulting in the requirement that she file a gift tax return.*

However, no taxes were due. All the gift did was reduce her $600,000 exemption to $360,000. Since she had no more property, this reduction will have no effect.

*   *   *

Sarah Jefferson had an estate worth $185,000. She was concerned about the cost of a prolonged nursing home stay and decided to give her assets to her four children. Because her estate was under $600,000, and she hadn't used any of her $600,000 exemption previously, there were no gift tax implications. Additionally, this money was not taxable to her children when they received it. However, there were nursing care implications, which are discussed in Chapters 24 and 25.

Estate reduction

Gifting is a very important part of estate planning, although it tends to be underutilized and misused. There are not many ways to reduce the value of your estate, but planned gifting is one. Used properly, gifting can be a valuable tax-reduction method.

Richard and Margaret Greene have an estate worth $8 million. They have sufficient income from their current investments and retirement plan and would like to reduce the size of their estate as much as possible. Since the Greenes have four children and 14 grandchildren, they can give $10,000 to each. Therefore, a continuing program of gifting will allow them to give a combined $360,000 per year. After 10 years, they will have reduced their estate by $3.6 million plus all the future growth in those assets.

You might consider giving away rapidly appreciating property. For example, if you have a piece of real estate that you feel will increase in value, you might gift it to a child to remove it from your estate. Upon your death, it will not be included in your estate for estate tax calculations. However, there are other considerations.

Cost basis

One involves the "cost basis," which is your cost of your property. Assume you bought a piece of real estate for $10,000. Upon sale, a capital gain, the difference between the sales price and the cost basis of $10,000, must be realized. There are two rules that apply to cost basis.

- If you give property away, the cost basis remains the same and is transferred to the recipient. Therefore, the recipient, upon sale of the property, will have income taxes on the difference between the sales price and the $10,000 cost basis.
- If you die and that property is inherited, the heir receives a "stepped-up basis." That means that the cost basis is not your cost basis of $10,000, but it "steps up" to the value at your death.

Let's compare these two scenarios.

Leon Farnsworth purchased land on the outskirts of town for $10,000. Over the years the property increased in value to $80,000. He gave it to his son Tommy. As you know by now, he made a gift of $70,000 (the $80,000 market value of the property less his $10,000 annual exemption). This had the effect of reducing his $600,000 exemption to $530,000. Tommy held it for a number of years and then sold it for $150,000. Tommy paid tax on the capital gain, which was the difference between the sales price and his cost basis. Since he received the property as a gift, his cost basis was the same as his father's, $10,000. That resulted in income tax on $140,000. On the other hand, Mr. Farnsworth was able to remove the appreciation of the property from his estate.

Now, let's look at what might have happened had Mr. Farnsworth instead chosen to hold the property. In this situation, we'll assume that it was worth $150,000 on the day Mr. Farnsworth died.

The property would have passed to Tommy, and he immediately could have sold it for $150,000. While there is normally capital gains tax on the difference between the sales price and the purchase price, in this case, there would have been none. Even though Tommy would have sold it for $150,000, that figure would have been his cost basis. When Mr. Farnsworth died, the cost basis of the property would have "stepped-up" from the original cost to the market value on the date of his death. As a result, there would have been no income tax due. However, the entire $150,000 would have been included in Mr. Farnsworth's estate for estate tax purposes.

One of the proposals floating around Washington is to eliminate the step-up at death benefit. This would be especially devastating to families who have land, businesses and securities that have been in their family for a long period of time.

Estate taxes versus income taxes

These scenarios point out the difficulty in the decision-making process. Estate taxes currently are higher than income taxes. In our planning, the relative value of income taxes compared to estate taxes must be considered. Would it have been better for Tommy to pay income taxes upon sale of the property while allowing his father to remove a substantial sum from his estate? Or should Mr. Farnsworth's estate have paid estate taxes on the entire amount but given Tommy a "stepped-up" basis? While there are too many variables to answer here, it is a factor that must be considered.

Under normal circumstances, it is better to pay income taxes rather than estate taxes. The *highest* income tax bracket is 39.6 percent; the *lowest* estate tax bracket is 37 percent. But your individual situation will still rule.

Notice, also, that you get the worst of all possible tax worlds with gifts. While the value of the gift is the value of the property on the day the gift is made ($80,000 in the previous case), the cost basis for the recipient remains at the basis of the donor ($10,000). The IRS gets you coming and going in this case.

Using your annual gift to create wealth

Many people use their $10,000 annual exclusion to reduce their estate, as reflected by the previous case. But all that will do in the Greenes' case is reduce their estate by $360,000 annually and create that amount for their children and grandchildren. As noted in the example, after 10 years, they will have reduced their estate by $3.6 million and created $3.6 million worth of wealth for their heirs.

But there is a better alternative.

Richard and Margaret Greene could have used that $360,000 per year to purchase a second-to-die insurance policy that is covered in the following chapters. Even if they had used only half their exclusions, or $180,000 per year, they could have purchased a $9,332,000 policy, using current projections! In 10 years, based on *today's assumptions, the death benefit on that policy would have grown to $11,666,450. Therefore, not only would they have reduced their estate by $1.8 million over 10 years, they would have created $11,666,450 worth of wealth for their children and grandchildren! And this is using only half their annual gift exclusions. To make it even better, if properly established, this amount would have been income tax-free and estate tax-free! If they lived another 20 years, they could create $15 million tax-free for their heirs! And, don't forget, if they die in the first year, the entire $9,332,000 would be paid.*

Of course, the children and grandchildren would have lost the benefit of half of the annual gifts. But they would have substantially increased their inheritance. Let's look at another case.

Ben and Nora Adams have an estate valued at $1.1 million. They are close to the $1.2 million combined cutoff ($600,000 each), so they have decided to start gifting some assets. They have three children, so together they could gift $60,000 per year. As long as their estate doesn't grow much, they should be in good shape from an estate tax standpoint. But they don't like the idea of giving up control of their assets to the children. And they know if they give them cash, the money will probably be wasted.

In the Adamses' case, they could purchase a $2.4 million second-to-die policy for $60,000 payable for 15 years. In 10 years, the death benefit would be over $3 million! You can see the leverage available by using life insurance.

If your goal is to make the fullest use of estate planning, doesn't it make sense to maximize your gift exemption? The wealth you can create is enormous. And by using the techniques covered in the following chapters, this money can be free of all taxes! What better legacy to leave?

Loan guarantees can result in taxable gifts

Here's a shocker: If you guarantee a loan for another person, it is subject to gift taxes.

Joan Malone wanted to help her son begin a new business. That business required $50,000 in operating capital. Unfortunately, her son didn't have that available, nor could he qualify for a loan.

However, Joan could qualify. Therefore, she went with him to the bank and guaranteed the loan. That innocent step resulted in a gift to her son of $40,000 (the amount over her annual $10,000 exclusion).

The IRS has recently ruled that guaranteeing a loan for the benefit of another results in a gift. This requires that a gift tax return be filed, thereby reducing the donor's $600,000 lifetime exemption by the amounts over the $10,000 annual exclusion. This is true even if the guarantee is never exercised.

Loan guarantees can result in additional estate taxes

Additionally, for married couples using the unlimited marital deduction discussed earlier, it causes even more potential problems. Normally, we just concern ourselves with the rule that for property to qualify for the unlimited marital deduction, the surviving spouse must receive income from that property annually. But there are a few other conditions. Among them: There must be nothing that will cause his or her interest in that property to end.

However, a loan guarantee represents a contingent liability. We don't know if it will ever be exercised. Upon the death of the guarantor, that guarantee doesn't end. It is passed on to the estate. Therefore, any money passed under the unlimited marital deduction may be needed to meet those guarantees. As a result, that property will be disqualified for the marital deduction and instead will be counted against the guarantor's $600,000 lifetime exemption.

This ruling can have dramatic effects on estate taxes. It can even disqualify a Q-TIP trust for the unlimited marital deduction. The ramifications are enormous, and there are no attractive solutions, other than providing sufficient liquidity in the estate and some careful, creative planning.

Putting property into joint tenancy

One problem that frequently occurs is the result of property being placed into joint tenancy with a non-spouse. We talked about the potential problems with joint tenancy earlier in the book. Remember, if you place property (stocks, bonds, real estate, etc.) into a joint account with a child, you are technically making a gift to the child. To make matters worse, the entire value of the property is included in your estate at your death. Talk about a no-win situation!

Conclusion

Gifting, while an important part of estate planning, is not the solution to all your problems. You still must give up control of the property, and when push comes to shove, many people don't want to do that. Nevertheless, if one of your goals is to reduce your estate taxes, and you have taken into consideration the income tax consequences for your recipients, then proper gifting can prove very valuable in the long run. Be sure to obtain qualified legal and financial advice.

Sixteen

How Can I Avoid Paying Estate Taxes on My Life Insurance?

If you are like most of my clients, you will probably be surprised to learn that, under most circumstances, life insurance proceeds are included in your estate when you die. Most people assume that since the proceeds are payable to someone else, they aren't included. Not true. Let's once again look at the Purcells.

> *The Purcells had a $2 million estate that included $750,000 of life insurance. Upon Mr. Purcell's death, $600,000 went into a family trust, while the balance went into the marital trust for Mrs. Purcell. Upon her death, all her property passed to their children with the amount over her $600,000 exemption subject to estate taxes. Because their estate included $750,000 worth of life insurance, they missed yet another tax-saving opportunity.*

Current rules

Ownership of life insurance. First, understand that there are two taxation issues when it comes to life insurance: income taxes and estate taxes. While life insurance proceeds are, under normal circumstances, *income tax-free*, they can be subject to *estate taxes*, depending on the size of your estate. It's all based on something known as "incidents of ownership."

According to the IRS, you have *incidents of ownership* in a policy if you maintain certain rights, such as changing the beneficiary or owner, pledging the policy as collateral, borrowing against or surrendering the policy, etc. The result of these "rights" is that the policy proceeds are included in your estate at your death.

In order to keep life insurance proceeds out of your estate at your death, you must either:

- Never have incidents of ownership in the policy, or
- Live at least three years after transferring the ownership to another party.

Ownership is the primary determination as to where the value of the death benefit falls.

Robert Marks borrowed $500,000 from Brittingham Bank and Trust to build an office. The bank required that Mr. Marks purchase a life insurance policy to cover the loan upon his death. When he died, the $500,000 death benefit was included in the value of his estate, although it didn't go to a family member. Of course, the value of his estate was increased by the elimination of the debt he owed the bank. Nevertheless, because he owned the policy, it was included in his estate.

An important point to remember is that if your estate is subject to estate taxes, and you are, for example, carrying a $500,000 insurance policy, your family might not realize the full benefit of the $500,000. They may only keep the amount that is left after estate taxes have been paid. The only way to receive full benefit from that policy is to make sure that neither you nor your spouse have any incidents of ownership.

Cross-ownership no longer an advantage. Before talking about how to do that, let's talk about what no longer works. For years, life insurance agents have told their clients that the husband should own the insurance carried by the wife, and the wife should own the insurance carried by the husband. The reason for this was, prior to the Economic Recovery Act of 1981, there were potential estate taxes at the death of the first spouse. Therefore, it made sense to get the proceeds of the life insurance out of the estate of the first to die. The result was a strategy that involved what was called "cross-ownership" of policies.

However, that strategy no longer saves estate taxes because there is no tax due at the first death if you take advantage of the unlimited marital deduction. Unfortunately, there are still many so-called "professionals" telling people that cross-ownership should be used to save estate taxes. So be aware of advisors who are still operating under old laws.

Third party ownership

Under current law, the most effective way to remove life insurance proceeds from the estate is to have the policy owned by someone other than the husband or wife. As long as neither the husband nor the wife have any "incidents of ownership," the proceeds will not be subject to estate taxes. For a single person, the same rules apply. As long as he or she doesn't own the policy, it will be excluded from his or her estate for tax purposes, subject to the three-year rule discussed below.

Transferring an existing policy. After hearing this, the first thought of many people is to transfer the ownership of their policy to another party. After all, given the choice between purchasing a new life insurance policy in which they have no incidents of ownership, and transferring the ownership of an existing policy, most people will choose the latter. Unfortunately, there is a problem with this tactic.

The previous tax laws included a special provision for gifts made "in contemplation of death." In a nutshell, it meant that any gift made within three years of the death of the donor was pulled back and included in his or her estate for tax purposes. The thinking of the Internal Revenue Service, rightly or wrongly, was that this gift was being made to allow the donor to reduce his or her estate tax liability. The Economic Recovery Tax Act of 1981 repealed this provision except in a few cases, one of which happens to be life insurance.

As a result, *the three-year rule still applies for life insurance.* If you transfer ownership of a life insurance contract within three years of your death, the death proceeds will be included in your estate for estate tax purposes. To put it another way, the only way to exempt a transferred policy from your estate is to retain no "incidents of ownership" three years prior to your death.

In 1987, Dr. William Bartels purchased, and was the owner of, a $500,000 policy. On Jan. 10, 1989 he removed it from his estate by gifting it to his son John. (There would have been gift tax problems had the policy contained cash value.) He died March 21, 1990. Since that was within three years of the transfer, the $500,000 was included in his estate.

This rule makes planning with existing life insurance very difficult. Though it would be great to transfer an existing life insurance policy, it is ludicrous to plan that you are not going to die within three years. If you know when you are going to die, then planning is easy. In my opinion, it is too risky to face the exposure of dying within three years and then having a substantial amount of estate taxes due.

Children as owners of your life insurance. To avoid the three-year rule, the prudent way to plan is to have another party own your policy from the beginning. One option that many of my clients choose is to make their adult child or children owners of the life insurance. As far as the IRS is concerned (at least today), if your children own your life insurance policy, and you never possessed any "incidents of ownership," then it will not be included in your estate for estate tax purposes, even if you die within three years. However, the IRS is always attempting to pull life insurance proceeds into the estate, so it is imperative to keep on top of recent rulings.

There are some *potential pitfalls* to having a child own your life insurance:

- The insurance becomes an asset of the child, and just as jointly owned property with a child causes problems, so does this. As his or her asset, any values can be attached in the event of a lawsuit, divorce, judgment, etc.
- If you want to provide income for your spouse from the proceeds of your insurance, then he or she would have to receive that money from the owner, which is the child. This, in turn, will create other problems. First, there is no guarantee the child will give the money to the parent, since it legally belongs to the child. Second, if he or she does give the money to the parent, this is considered a gift. Making your spouse the beneficiary won't work because then the money will be included in his or her estate at death, and that is what you were trying to avoid in the first place.
- If a child is an owner, there is no guarantee that he or she won't cash in the policy early.
- If you pay the premiums directly on a policy owned by others, there can be gift tax implications on the payments over your $10,000 annual exclusion.

A trust as owner of your insurance. Because of the problems stated previously, the solution in many cases is to have your life insurance owned by an *irrevocable life insurance trust*. If handled properly, you should not run into any of the problems we have discussed.

Although the use of an irrevocable trust is more cumbersome and involves more steps than any other method, I believe it is the prudent fashion for owning life insurance. It complies with the IRS regulation that states that a life insurance policy not owned or paid for by an individual will not be included in his or her estate. Let's go through this process step by step.

- An attorney drafts an irrevocable trust. For safety's sake, it is recommended that you not even call it a life insurance trust.
- A trustee and successor trustees are named. These people should definitely not be either you or your spouse. Many attorneys recommend that you not name one of the beneficiaries as a trustee, either. The safest course of action is to have a disinterested third party—a financial institution, your CPA, etc.—as trustee.
- You gift an amount slightly larger than the life insurance premium to the trust. This gift is made under your $10,000 gift exclusion. This gift will be considered a "present interest" gift if you use the "Crummey provisions" (from Crummey vs. IRS, 1968), which are described shortly. These payments may be made annually or in one single payment.
- Upon your death (or the deaths of you and your spouse if it is a joint trust), the proceeds are paid to the beneficiaries estate tax-free, assuming everything has been handled properly.

There are some *disadvantages* with the use of the trust.

- The trust is irrevocable. Once you have made the gift, you cannot get it back. The values that build in the policy belong to the trust, not you.
- It is complicated and involves specific steps under the "Crummey provisions."

- It must be drafted by an estate planning attorney who understands the intricacies.
- There can be some gift tax implications between the beneficiaries based on the gift made to the trust.
- This trust has a separate federal identification number and, if it shows taxable earnings, must file an income tax return.

There are some basic decisions you must make in structuring your insurance trust.

- Is it going to be a single or joint trust? A single trust is used when: 1) you are not married; or 2) the surviving spouse is going to have a need for the insurance benefits. A joint trust is used when the primary purpose of the proceeds is to pay estate taxes.
- If your purpose is to provide for your spouse without having the proceeds included in either of your estates, there are very strict rules that must be followed. These parallel the rules governing the family trust discussed earlier.
- Who will be the ultimate beneficiaries, and what will be their rights? As a rule, the terms of this trust follow the terms of the living trust for continuity.

The Crummey provisions

Discussing the Crummey provisions might fall under the category of "telling you more than you want to know," but it is a vital part of the irrevocable insurance trust. As discussed in the previous chapter, in order for a gift to qualify under the $10,000 annual exclusion, it must be a "present interest." That means that the recipient must have full and unrestricted use of that gift today, with no strings attached.

The problem with life insurance is the nature of the trust. In an irrevocable trust, the interests of the beneficiaries are *future interests*. That is because they have no current rights in the policy. All the "incidents of ownership" are vested in the trustee. That means that the gift will not qualify as a "present interest" gift.

Therefore, to make it "present interest," specific steps must be taken. Those steps fall under the Crummey provision, aptly named after the landmark case, Crummey vs. IRS (1968). Without getting technical, it involves the following steps (see Exhibit 5).

1. You gift the premiums to the trustee of the trust.
2. The trustee then notifies the beneficiaries (presumably your children) in writing of the gift and gives them a limited time (usually 30 days) to withdraw the premiums.
3. The beneficiaries then sign a waiver declining the money.
4. Once the trustee has received this waiver, he or she then pays the premiums to the insurance company.

According to the IRS, that withdrawal privilege given to the beneficiaries is sufficient to allow the money to qualify for a "no strings" gift.

Keep in mind, however, that the IRS is constantly challenging estates to bring the life insurance proceeds into the estate. Nevertheless, they haven't won a case where the trust was properly established and the necessary procedures followed. So it is imperative that you only work with qualified professionals who stay abreast of the constant changes in IRS regulations. Otherwise, it could cost your estate hundreds of thousands, or millions, in estate taxes.

Benefits of the insurance trust

Let's assume we can bring the Purcells back from the grave and pretend they planned differently.

> *The Purcells' estate, valued at $2 million, included a $750,000 life insurance policy on the life of Mr. Purcell, owned from the beginning by an irrevocable trust. This resulted in the $750,000 being excluded from their estate. This had the effect of reducing their taxable estate to $1,250,000. Upon Mr. Purcell's death, $600,000 of his property went into a family trust, the balance went into the marital trust for Mrs. Purcell. When she died, she passed $650,000 to her children, with only $50,000 subject to estate taxes. The balance of the estate, ($1,981,500) passed estate tax-free! The resulting taxes were only $18,500.*

This $18,500 is a far cry from the $320,000 their children had to pay when their life insurance was included in their estate. Exhibit 6 shows a diagram of this amazing tax savings.

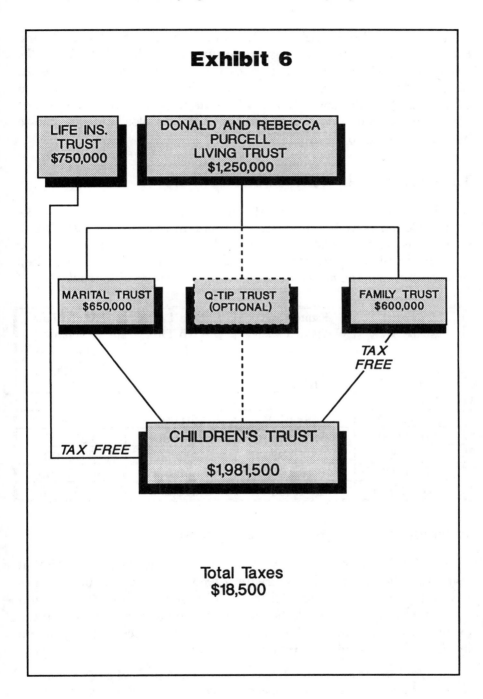

Exhibit 6

LIFE INS. TRUST
$750,000

DONALD AND REBECCA PURCELL LIVING TRUST
$1,250,000

MARITAL TRUST
$650,000

Q-TIP TRUST
(OPTIONAL)

FAMILY TRUST
$600,000

TAX FREE

CHILDREN'S TRUST
$1,981,500

TAX FREE

Total Taxes
$18,500

Let's recap the financial results of our planning for Mr. and Mrs. Purcell. *We have reduced their estate taxes from $561,180 under the simple will, to $18,500 using various planning methods.* As a result, we have increased the amount of their children's inheritance from $1,379,220 to $1,981,500. Not bad for a day's work! Can you see now why I feel so good about my profession? Where else is it possible to help people save so much money so easily?

Tax savings with a life insurance trust

The following table shows the net estate taxes for various scenarios. Column one is the estate size; column two the *net estate taxes* without use of the credit equivalent; column three the *net estate taxes* with the family trust (or other use of the exemption of the first-to-die); and column four the *net estate taxes* using the irrevocable trust.

Current Estate Size	Estate Taxes Without Family Trust	Estate Taxes With The Family Trust	Estate Tax With Insurance Trust
1,000,000	153,000	0	0
1,500,000	363,000	114,000	0
2,000,000	588,000	320,000	18,500
3,000,000	1,098,000	784,000	430,500
4,000,000	1,648,000	1,318,000	912,500
5,000,000	2,198,000	1,868,000	1,455,500
10,000,000	4,948,000	4,618,000	4,205,000

Incredible leverage with life insurance

One of the primary advantages of an irrevocable trust is that it gives you the opportunity to create a tremendous dollar pool that is *federal income tax-free, state income tax-free, federal estate tax-free, and state inheritance tax-free.* Although we talk about the $10,000 annual exclusion, you are not limited to that figure. By exceeding it, you can multiply the value of your $600,000 exemption.

Richard and Juanita Mason had an estate valued at $1.8 million. Richard's retirement income was such that he didn't need any

140

of the principal to provide for himself and his family. In fact, he was reinvesting all the interest from his investments, which was causing his estate to grow. Richard was an astute businessman, very much aware of estate tax consequences. He was intrigued by the leverage of the life insurance trust, but didn't want to commit himself to annual payments. He said he would feel more comfortable just investing a lump sum of $100,000.

The following table shows the Mason's alternatives using current projections. They could have left the $100,000 in tax-free bonds earning 5 percent and continued to reinvest the interest at that rate, or they could have transferred $100,000 into a life insurance contract providing a $600,000 initial death benefit. The death benefit could then grow annually as the cash values inside the policy grew. Both sets of figures assume the investment is in an irrevocable trust.

Year of Death	Value of Tax-Free Bonds In a Trust	Value of Life Insurance In a Trust
5	127,628	506,373
10	162,889	548,864
15	207,893	601,563
20	265,330	659,242
25	338,635	717,701

As you can see, the $100,000 created tremendous leverage when used for life insurance. And, don't forget, we don't know when they are going to die. One thing about the insurance, it is guaranteed to pay the death benefit, even if they die immediately. Their other investments won't do that.

One note about the single deposit. Since the Masons used the Crummey provisions described earlier, they were each able to gift $10,000 to each of their two sons. Nevertheless, there was still a $60,000 ($30,000 each) overage that came off each of their $600,000 lifetime exemptions. But the use of that $60,000 created an unbelievable return-on-investment that is both income and estate tax-free for their sons. Nothing can do it better.

Caution

One word of caution here. As they say on television, "Don't try this at home." The techniques described in this chapter are not the kinds of procedures you should do on your own without professional advice. Make sure you are working with both a competent estate planning attorney and a life insurance professional who understand the intricacies of insurance trusts and generation skipping. The laws concerning irrevocable trusts and Crummey powers are very strict and complete. If this isn't handled properly, the IRS dragon will jump all over you and pull the entire proceeds of the life insurance into your estate...which is exactly what they would like to do.

Seventeen

How Can I Substantially Reduce My Estate Tax Cost?

In previous chapters, we have discussed various ways to reduce estate taxes: the use of trusts; gifting money out of your estate; the life insurance trust; and generation skipping. Nevertheless, even after these steps have been taken, additional estate taxes may be due. How will they be paid?

Remember, in most cases, estate taxes are due at the death of the second spouse. Your CPA calculates the gross estate, reduces it by any liabilities and credits, and arrives at the tax. *That tax must be paid within nine months.*

Paying estate taxes

Charles and Ruth Webster have an estate that is projected to be nearly $4 million at the second death. Of that value, approximately $1 million consists of a business owned by Charles. Even after taking advantage of each of their $600,000 exemptions, their children will still have an estate tax bill of $1,318,000.

That is a lot of money to send to Uncle Sam! Mr. Webster's business needs to gross $19 million to *net* $1.3 million. Where will the tax money come from? Let's look at the alternatives.

1. Use **cash.** Their children could send the IRS $1,318,000 in cash from their inheritance (if they have it). If not, they could have to liquidate assets.
2. **Borrow** the money. The heirs might be able to go to a bank and borrow $1,318,000.

3. Pay in **installments.** Since the Websters' estate meets the qualifications of Internal Revenue Codes Section 6166, the heirs could pay the IRS in installments.

4. Pay with **discounted dollars.** Instead of forcing his children to pay $1,318,000, Mr. Webster could pay 10 percent of that amount, in advance, over a period of years. This technique, which involves life insurance, can reduce the cost of his estate taxes by 90 percent!

Let's look at each alternative in detail, exploring the advantages and disadvantages of each.

Cash

Most estates can pay the taxes with available cash. The Websters' estate should have sufficient liquidity, either in cash or assets, with which to pay the taxes. However, there are several disadvantages to this.

- They must pay 100 cents on the dollar. While this might not sound so bad now, I believe it will be less attractive as you continue this chapter. I will show you a way to reduce the cost of your estate taxes to the point that it could cost only *10 or 20 cents on the dollar!*

- If they have to liquidate assets (sell stock, bonds, real estate, business property, etc.), there is no guarantee that they won't have to sell more than $1,318,000 worth of property to raise that much cash. Forcing a quick sale usually means accepting less than full value. Additionally, the stock or real estate markets may be down or the country may be in a recession. Any number of things could make this extremely difficult or displeasing. In this case, it could easily cost more than 100 cents on the dollar.

Borrow

It amazes me the number of people who assume their heirs will be able to go to a bank and borrow the money with which to pay their estate taxes. They presume that since the estate has assets, a financial institution will jump at the chance to lend them the money.

It goes without saying how financial institutions feel about lending money today. It's not easy to borrow, under the best of circumstances. While it is possible that there may be sufficient assets to use as collateral, you would need a very friendly banker. And even if the money could be borrowed, it would result in substantial interest.

We don't know what the banking situation will be when the Websters' children are faced with estate taxes. But we do know that we can't depend on the banks to finance their estate taxes. And we will see shortly that borrowing is, in fact, the most expensive of the various alternatives.

Installment plan

The IRS, being the kind organization that it is, allows for an installment plan to be used in two situations.

Section 6161. Rarely, the IRS may grant the heirs an extension of up to 10 years if they can be convinced that there are sufficient reasons for not paying the taxes. For its part, the IRS has certain guidelines that must be met. In addition to the interest, a bond may be required. Although this sounds good, we'll see how costly it can be.

Section 6166. This section is used when the value of a closely held business or farm exceeds 35 percent of the adjusted gross estate. If the Websters still qualify at their death, their estate taxes could be paid over a period of up to 14 years, with the first four being interest only. Interest at a rate of 4 percent would be added, which could double the cost. Besides the heavy interest charges, there are a few other disadvantages. First, the IRS can hold a lien on their property. This can result in some obvious problems. Second, the reduced interest rate applies only to the first $1 million of business value. Third, any gifts made within three years of death can be pulled back into the estate for calculation purposes. Fourth, a bond may be required. Fifth, since only a portion of the estate taxes can usually qualify, cash is still required. Finally, there are a myriad of rules and regulations that make this plan difficult.

While the IRS has made a valid attempt at helping people allow their heirs to keep their businesses, it is still an expensive alternative. There is still a much better way, and that involves the use of *discounting* the cost of your estate taxes with life insurance.

Life insurance

Some of my clients hate to talk about life insurance. They don't like insurance agents; they don't like the premiums. That is OK with me. I hate doctor bills, too. But that doesn't mean I am going to avoid doctors, especially if I want to enjoy a long and healthy life. Life insurance, too, is necessary if you want to maximize your assets and provide for your family.

The truth is that life insurance companies provide a benefit nobody else can match. They accept relatively small amounts of dollars from you (premiums) and guarantee to pay large amounts of dollars (death proceeds) to your beneficiaries. That doesn't sound so bad to me.

The problem with life insurance is not the product, but the way it has been sold. Historically, the industry has attracted some poorly qualified men and women. With the enormous number of agents and so many companies, it is difficult to ensure that each salesperson is properly trained and qualified. After all, you don't have to be a rocket scientist to get an insurance license. As a result, most agents are unaware of the intricacies of the estate planning market.

On the other hand, there are some unbelievably qualified agents representing fantastic insurance companies. The job, therefore, is to separate the wheat from the chaff, and that is not always easy. But don't condemn an entire industry for the actions of a few. Life insurance is too important for that.

Over the years, many of my clients have passed away. And do you know what? Not one widow refused the life insurance check. Not one advisor told his client's family that they really didn't need all that insurance money. Not one child told me to send the money back. Life insurance is the consummate unselfish act. You are providing a special benefit for your loved ones, and that is very generous.

Massive dollars when needed. Life insurance can do for your family what no other product can do: guarantee substantial dollars when they are needed most. Can your investment in Xerox do that? Can your real estate investments do that? Can your retirement plan do that? Can your CDs do that? No. None of these investments can *guarantee* massive dollars when they are needed...unless you invest massive dollars. But life insurance can provide the big bucks when they are needed most. That is why it is such an invaluable planning tool.

Life insurance to pay estate taxes. Referring to the Webster case, the children will need $1.3 million with which to pay estate taxes. We have looked at the alternatives, none of which involves paying less than $1.3 million. But my job is to help you reduce your outlay for estate taxes. So let's look closely at the last alternative, life insurance.

Mr. Webster could purchase a $1 million policy that, using current projections, would have a death benefit that increases each year until it reaches $1,318,000 in the 20th year, the projected date of the second death. The annual premium for that amount of insurance would be approximately $12,000 for 20 years, or $240,000 if he lives that long.

But there is an even better way to fill the need. It is a relatively new type of coverage called a *"second-to-die"* policy. Since estate taxes aren't due until the second spouse dies, prudent planning would suggest buying a policy that won't pay until that occurrence. By insuring both parties with a policy that pays at the second death, you take advantage of joint mortality for a reduced premium.

In the Webster's case, a premium of under $6,000 per year for 20 years would fund a policy that, using current projections, would also have a death benefit of $1,318,000 in 20 years. This is less than half of the cost of the policy on Mr. Webster alone. An investment of $120,000 over 20 years, assuming the Websters live that long, can provide over $1.3 million, *estate and income tax-free!*

Choices in paying taxes

Let's review the alternatives by looking at actual dollars (See Exhibit 7).

1. Pay cash of $1,318,000.
2. Borrow the money at 8 percent per year for 10 years, for a total cost of $1,964,210.
3. Use Section 6166, paying interest only for four years and then amortizing the balance over 10 more years, for a total cost of $1,636,257.

4. Purchase insurance, with an initial premium of $6,000 for 20 years (present dollars) for a maximum of $120,000, using current projections.

For me the choice is easy. Paying $120,000 beats $1,318,000, $1,964,210 or $1,636,257 any day of the week. Why would anyone choose any of the other alternatives?

The insurance doubters among you have all kinds of reasons why you shouldn't use life insurance. Let's answer some of those questions.

How about the net present value of the money?

Good question. Although premiums must be paid starting today, death benefits won't be paid until sometime in the future. Therefore, you can't compare paying $120,000 starting today with $1,318,000 paid in maybe 20 years.

That may be correct. That is why I provided the lower part of Exhibit 7. While the top half of the page reflects the total cost of paying $1,318,000, the bottom half shows the net present value. And, as you can see, insurance is still the cheapest source of dollars.

Can't we invest the money and receive a higher rate?

Although it is possible, there are two reasons why this is highly unlikely.

- If the Websters want that same return in another type of investment, they will need to earn *28.63 percent after taxes* on that same $6,000 investment for 20 years. In their tax bracket, that would be an earnings rate of 43 percent before taxes, which is virtually impossible. Don't forget, there are no income taxes on the growth of the cash value in a life insurance policy. Additionally, they would have had to put this fantastic investment in an irrevocable trust, like the life insurance, to remove it from their estate.
- Even if they could find such an investment, will that investment *guarantee them $1 million if they die the first year?* Of course not. Life insurance is unique because it is the only investment that can guarantee a large amount of money

from day one. Since our date of death is unknown, nothing else can possibly work as well.

Why should I worry? I've got a lot of years to go.

You hope you do. But let's be realistic. What is to guarantee that you won't die tomorrow? Everybody is in good health until the day comes that he or she is no longer in good health. How can you possibly know what that day is for you? No one plans to be killed in an accident. Maybe it's tomorrow; maybe it's 40 years from now. Maybe you want to take that chance, but I don't. Proper planning should not be a game of Russian Roulette. You are going to die. That's guaranteed. Why not also guarantee that no matter when that day comes, your family will not suffer financially?

Why not pay my estate taxes in cash? I have the money.

What if the Websters have that money sitting in the bank or in liquid assets? Why should they bother with life insurance since the children will have sufficient cash with which to pay the estate taxes?

That philosophy totally misses the point. Whether or not they have the cash is irrelevant. The fact is they are going to lose nearly 33 percent of their estate in taxes! What difference does it make whether they have that 33 percent sitting in the bank? Don't you think they would like to pay those taxes with the cheapest dollars possible? The Websters have spent a lifetime building that estate. Why should they throw one-third of it away needlessly? Using the methods in this chapter, they can reduce the cost of their estate taxes from 33 percent of their estate to 3 percent! Why in the world wouldn't they want to do that and leave their heirs with a greater gift?

Why can't I just buy term insurance?

This is another excellent question. After all, over a 20-year period, isn't term insurance usually less expensive than ordinary insurance? Well, yes and no. While over a 20-year period term insurance might be less expensive than a policy on Mr. Webster's life only, it will likely be more expensive than a second-to-die policy. But cost isn't the only factor. There are two other considerations.

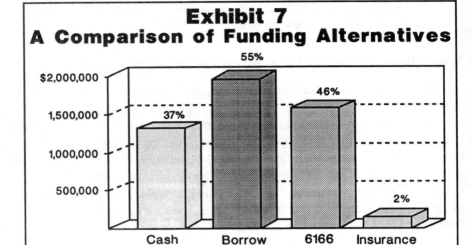

Exhibit 7
A Comparison of Funding Alternatives

Cash:	$1,318,000	
Borrow:	At 8% ten annual payments of $196,421 would total $1,964,210.	
IRC Section 6166:	Immediate cash need at death of $938,173 plus interest payments of $31,071 each year for four years, then principal and interest payments of $57,380 for ten years for a total of $1,636,257.	
Insurance:	Initial premiums of $6,000 for twenty years for a total of $120,000.	

NET PRESENT VALUE*		
	Total	Cost of One Dollar
Cash	$340,596	$1.00
Borrow	356,509	1.05
IRC 6166	349,092	1.02
Insurance	68,014	0.20

* Calculated at 7.00% over 20 years

1. We don't know when the Websters are going to die. If the purpose of this insurance is to pay estate taxes, which it is, and Mr. Webster purchases a term policy, what happens if the insurance expires before he does? If you look at insurance industry statistics, most term insurance never results in a death claim; it usually lapses before the insured dies.
2. Term insurance has a nasty habit of getting increasingly expensive. While term insurance is cheap at younger ages, it gets prohibitive at older ages. And, remember, our purpose is to pay the estate taxes. What happens if Mr. or Mrs. Webster lives to age 80? They will no longer be able to afford term insurance. If the insurance is no longer in force, how will their heirs pay the estate taxes? We're back to square one because term insurance is only a temporary solution to a permanent problem.

What if the annual premium is over my gift tax exclusion?

Bobby Anderson has one primary goal: He wants to leave his entire $5 million estate to his children, estate tax-free. He has worked hard for the past 30 years and wants his children to receive every penny from his efforts. It sickened him when he was told that if he were to die today, *almost 45 percent of his hard work would go to the government* as estate taxes. To resolve this, his estate planning team recommended that Mr. Anderson purchase a $2.2 million life insurance policy and place it in an irrevocable trust. To fund the policy, he would transfer $40,000 per year for 10 years from his assets to the irrevocable trust. However, he has only two children. That means that by gifting that amount of money, he will exceed his $10,000 annual exclusion by $20,000 per year for 10 years.

But that is not much of a problem. His children will receive a much greater benefit from his using the additional $20,000 to buy insurance than they would if they inherited that much. The only consequence will be a reduction of his $600,000 exclusion by the overage. Nevertheless, his children will get the death benefit—$5 million, or 100 percent of his estate, free of taxes! As a result, he will have turned $200,000 of his $600,000 exclusion into $2.2 million, estate and income tax-free! In other words, $200,000 will do the work of $2.2 million.

The only logical solution

Looking at this logically, not emotionally, there is no other choice. It's a pure business decision. No matter what your bias, life insurance is the best solution to this problem.

Roger Borders hated life insurance. He hated agents. He hated premiums. But he realized he needed to do some planning. He warned me, "Lots of insurance agents are bugging me. While I want to do some planning, I don't want to buy any life insurance. The only reason I'm willing to talk to you is because of your reputation and the fact that you're not just an insurance agent." I said, "No problem. I won't mention life insurance."

At our first meeting, we discussed his particular problems. At the time, he owned a business, some real estate and had an estate of approximately $1.3 million. Again, he said that he wasn't interested in any life insurance. We held another meeting, this time with his wife and attorney. I presented a computer analysis of their potential tax liability. The analysis showed a future estate tax liability of approximately $300,000, based on conservative assumptions of growth, inflation and life expectancy. He said, "Where in the world are my kids going to get that kind of money without selling our assets? Nothing we have is liquid." I replied, "I could tell you, but I agreed not to, because it involves the 'L' word, and you don't want to hear it."

His wife jumped in, "Oh, yes, we do." I told them that at their ages, for $4,000 a year for approximately 10 years (based on then-current projections), they could invest in a second-to-die policy that would provide the needed $300,000 cash for their kids. But we also looked at all the alternatives as outlined previously. I showed him the cost breakdown of each method of payment. Being a successful businessman and realizing that there were no acceptable options, he chose to pay his taxes with the discounted dollars provided by insurance.

The attraction of life insurance is not that it is such a great investment. The enticement is a result of the fact that the life insurance industry operates under favorable tax laws. Used properly, life insurance has four primary advantages.

1. Cash values, unlike most investments, grow *tax deferred*. No income taxes have to be paid on the earnings.

2. Death benefits are paid *income tax-free*, under most circumstances.

3. If properly established in an irrevocable life insurance trust, or with third-party ownership, the growth and death benefits will also be *estate tax-free*.

4. The proceeds, if paid to a named beneficiary, are generally *free from the creditors* of the insured.

Conclusion

I don't want to sound like an insurance salesman trying to shove life insurance down your throat, because that is not the intention. Believe me, if there existed a real estate or stock market investment in which you could invest $4,000 and be guaranteed $300,000 immediately, income and estate tax-free, I would recommend it. But there is no other investment, when used properly, like life insurance. The key is to work with a professional who can show you how to use insurance to *your* advantage.

If you truly want to minimize all taxes and preserve the estate you have worked so hard to create, then properly structured life insurance may be part of the solution. So forget how you feel about it—look at the benefits.

Eighteen

What Should be My Concerns When Buying Life Insurance?

The insurance industry has undergone substantial changes in recent years. Because of the importance life insurance plays in estate planning, it is critical that we review the areas that can cause financial problems.

Twenty-five years ago, when I first entered the financial industry, this discussion would not have been as vital as it is today. In those years, there were few concerns about the safety of life insurance companies. However, all that has changed. With the recent failures in the insurance industry, it is imperative that we evaluate each and every life insurance company we are considering and choose only those that are conservative and stable.

There are approximately 1,800 life insurance companies and seemingly 18 million agents, most of whom seem to be calling or sending you information daily. You obviously don't have the time, or inclination, to talk to all these people. If you did, you wouldn't have time to work or run your business. On the other hand, it is vital to work with a competent life insurance professional, whether it is a life insurance agent or a financial planner.

Quality of the company

Though there are many life insurance companies, only a relative handful are what I consider worthy of recommendation to my clients. You have seen and heard the stories about the companies that have been seized by state insurance commissioners or forced into bankruptcy. We can assume there will be more problems in the future.

This is precisely what you want to *avoid* when buying a life insurance policy. Safety must be your primary concern!

Rating Services

Unless you are a financial analyst familiar with the insurance industry, you have to depend on rating services to do your work for you. At present, there are five major services.

A.M. Best and Company is the oldest insurance company rating service. It rates insurance companies as follows: A++ and A+ (Superior); A and A- (Excellent); B++ and B+ (Very Good); B and B- (Good); C++ and C+ (Fairly Good); C and C- (Marginal); D (Below Minimum Standards); E (Under State Supervision); and F (In Liquidation).

Standard and Poor's rates the claims-paying ability for approximately 250 companies and provides solvency ratings for about 700 companies. In my opinion, the solvency ratings don't have much value. However, the claims-paying ability ratings are valid and important. Those ratings are: AAA (Superior), AA+, AA and AA- (Excellent), A+, A and A- (Good), BBB+, BBB and BBB- (Adequate) and as low as D. Because Standard and Poor's charges anywhere from $15,000 to $28,000 per year, only the higher-quality companies tend to get rated. As a result, all but a few are rated A- or better.

Moody's Investor Service rates approximately 90 companies for financial strength. The ratings are Aaa (Exceptional), Aa (Excellent), A (Good), Baa (Adequate), Ba (Questionable), and as low as C. Moody's charges $25,000 per year for this services. Again, since only the higher-quality companies are willing to pay for this rating, most get rated A or better.

Duff and Phelps, Inc. rates the claims-paying ability of approximately 160 life insurance companies. Their rating grades parallel Standard & Poor's. Its service costs the insurance company $17,000, and again, virtually every company is A- or better.

Weiss Research is a relatively new service that rates approximately 1,100 insurance companies and sells those ratings to the general public. Its ratings are A+, A and A- (Excellent), B+, B and B-

(Good), C+, C and C- (Fair), D+, D and D- (Weak), E (Very Weak) and F (Failed). Unlike the other services, Weiss comes down hard on the insurance industry, placing 70 percent of the rated companies in the "C+" to "D-" range.

Although the insurance industry has gone through difficult times over the past several years, there are people who are trying to take advantage of this in a way not beneficial to the policyholder. You need to take what you read with a grain of salt. Although there have been a few failures, they represent a minor portion of the industry. As a rule, the industry is strong. They have come through the junk-bond and real estate failures, Hurricane Andrew and the 1993 floods fairly well. Virtually all the strong companies have survived. Nevertheless, you still must take care in choosing your companies. What you want is an insurance company that has conservative management, stability and superior strength.

In my practice, I feel comfortable working only with those companies that have an "A++" or "A+" rating from A. M. Best *in addition* to at least an AA rating from one or more of the other services. Since all major companies are rated by A.M. Best, you can easily find that rating. You can get the ratings from your insurance agent from your local library.

I recommend that when purchasing large amounts of insurance, you diversify between different companies. The reason for this is two-fold. First, for safety reasons, it makes sense to spread the risk. But, even more important, you don't know which companies will perform best over the years. They all differ in their investment policy. As a result, the amount of interest they credit to their policyholders will vary. By using different companies, you aren't placing all your eggs in one insurance basket.

Knowledge of the agent

Picking an agent is difficult, especially since most people aren't aware of an agent's competency until it's too late. While most agents are honest, hard-working people who want to do what is best for their clients, the majority are not familiar with complex estate planning concepts.

Scrutinize the agent. Are you compatible? Does he or she share your values? Ask the right questions? Listen to your answers? Does he

156

or she want to help you solve your problems first or just try to get you to buy a policy? Does he or she know the insurance business enough to help you, or do you have to do some educating? Does he or she want to work with other professionals (attorneys, CPAs) or do it all alone? Be careful, because we are talking about large dollars riding on his advice.

Common mistakes to avoid

Historically, many choices regarding insurance have been left to chance. There has been a lack of good advice and information for the insurance-buying public. This has resulted in a plethora of needless mistakes. Let's look at a few.

Proceeds payable to minors. We have previously discussed the problems with making a minor the beneficiary of your life insurance policy. I think it goes without saying at this point that it should be avoided. Instead, consider using a trust as beneficiary of your insurance proceeds.

Proceeds payable to your estate. It is amazing how many people make their estate the beneficiary of their life insurance. In my opinion, this is one of the worst mistakes you can make. There is virtually no advantage in naming the estate as beneficiary, other than it is simple and requires no thought. However, there are significant, expensive disadvantages.

- The insurance proceeds, which are, as a rule, creditor-free when paid to a named beneficiary, become subject to the creditors of the insured when paid to his or her estate.
- The proceeds, which avoid probate when paid to a named beneficiary, must go through probate when paid to the estate of the insured.
- The proceeds will be included in the estate of the insured for estate tax purposes, regardless of who owns the policy.
- The proceeds will pass according to the insured's will, and that raises the various problems that were covered earlier.

Ownership by the wrong party. The owner, not the insured, controls the policy. While you might want to make someone else the owner for financial reasons, understand the ramifications. It takes complete control out of your hands. However, there is a very good reason for removing the insurance proceeds from your estate: saving your heirs potentially hundreds of thousands of dollars in estate taxes.

Don't forget what I said earlier about cross-ownership of policies. It is no longer advantageous for the wife to own the husband's insurance, or vice versa. To remove it from both of your estates, it must be owned by an independent third party, such as an irrevocable trust or a child.

Indiscriminate changing of ownership. Changing the ownership of a policy, while easy to do, brings in all the dragons, with income, gift, and estate tax ramifications.

When Bernard Madison went into business, his life insurance agent suggested that his corporation purchase and own a policy on his life. Over the years, the policy built up substantial cash values. One day, on the advice of his agent, he transferred ownership of the policy from the corporation to himself. When he did that, the cash value in the policy became income to him personally and resulted in a significant tax liability.

*　　*　　*

Chris Boyd owned a $250,000 life insurance policy on himself that had $50,000 in cash value. To remove it from his estate, he transferred the ownership to his son Rudy. That immediately created a gift of the cash value. Additionally, when Chris died two years later, the entire $250,000 was included in his estate because he died within three years of transferring the ownership to Rudy.

Relying on inflated projections

As you review insurance proposals, remember they are based on current interest rate and mortality assumptions (as are the figures used throughout this book). Both can and will change over the years.

One caution about interest rates. We saw what happened in the savings and loan industry: those institutions that offered the highest rates took the highest risks. Of course, the consumer didn't care since the deposits were insured. Well, you don't have that luxury with life insurance. Be skeptical of unusually high rates. Don't get caught in the trap of "rate chasing."

State guaranty funds

There is currently concern about the financial stability of a few companies. Even with the current problems, the insurance industry has a very enviable record of protecting policyholders' assets. One mechanism in place to provide additional protection are the state guaranty funds. While not government-backed bank insurance, these funds do guarantee deposits with insurance companies. They are funded by the companies who sell insurance in each state and are designed to protect the policyholders residing in that state. The funds have the power to assess the companies if large claims arise. The benefits paid, however, are limited and vary from state to state. The majority of the funds provide coverage up to $300,000 in death benefits, $100,000 in cash values, and $100,000 for annuities.

One reason you don't hear much about these funds is that insurance agents aren't allowed to tell you about them. The states don't want to be in a position where agents, and policy purchasers, ignore the safety of a company because they know that there is insurance. They know what happened in the savings and loan industry, and they don't want agents to use that guarantee as a sales tool. As a result, most people don't hear about these until there is an insurance company failure.

When you purchase life insurance, make your choice as if there were no protection from outside forces. Make sure the company is highly rated based on the services discussed earlier. Then, hopefully, you will never find yourself in a position of relying on a guaranty fund.

Conclusion

The insurance industry provides a needed service to us all. Unfortunately, unscrupulous sales practices by some agents have given it a bad name. But insurance can still do things that other financial vehicles cannot. By exercising care and caution, you can enjoy its benefits without experiencing its pitfalls.

Nineteen

How Can Charitable Giving Reduce My Taxes and Increase My Income?

Over the years, Americans have been generous with charitable donations. We have given unselfishly to churches, synagogues, health organizations, medical foundations, hospitals, colleges and other charitable organizations. This has provided us with tax deductions as well as good feelings from helping others.

Recently, a new light has been shed on charitable giving, one that provides even greater benefits. As a result, charitable giving is a planning field unto itself. It is an integral part of estate planning that creates all kinds of opportunities for everybody involved.

Charitable giving is a legitimate practice when handled responsibly. If you are going to get involved in charitable giving, remember there are many IRS rules that are just waiting to trip you. Nevertheless, the opportunities are endless. You'll be amazed by the benefits.

Legitimate charities

Over the years, many groups have passed themselves off as genuine charities, of which many were frauds. While we are usually familiar with what is a legitimate charity, the IRS has made it easy for us by publishing a list of qualified charities.

Types of giving programs

There are several techniques that can be used for charitable giving. Four of the primary methods are:

1. **Charitable remainder annuity trust,** which provides a fixed income stream to a noncharitable beneficiary (for example the donor and his spouse) for a period of time, after which the property creating the income goes to the charity.

2. **Pooled income fund,** in which a donor's gift is combined with the gifts of others and provides a stream of income to the donor.

3. **Charitable lead trust,** which provides a flow of income to a charity for a certain number of years, after which the trust ends, and the property reverts to a noncharitable beneficiary.

4. **Charitable remainder unitrust,** the discussion of which follows.

Charitable remainder unitrust

The charitable remainder unitrust (CRUT) is the most flexible of the various charitable trusts. The type of CRUT that I think is best-suited to the individual needs of most people is the "net income unitrust with a makeup provision." Let's look at this form of CRUT and see how it might be used.

A net income unitrust with makeup provision is a type of charitable remainder unitrust into which you gift property that will go to a charity upon the death of you and your spouse. In the meantime, you have the opportunity to receive the income from that trust in addition to a number of other benefits outlined below. The CRUT has become extremely popular with people because it offers flexibility and a variety of benefits that cannot be achieved elsewhere.

- The CRUT can be used as a supplement for a qualified retirement plan.

- It can permit you to sell appreciated assets without having to pay capital gains taxes.

- It can protect assets from lawsuits.

- With the CRUT, you can receive benefits now while leaving money to a qualified charity later.

- You can reduce estate taxes by moving assets into a CRUT.

Parties to the trust. A CRUT is irrevocable, which means you can't change the terms (although there are a few things you can change, as we'll see later). Like all trusts, it has a *trustmaker* (you), a *trustee* (can be you or another person), an *administrator* (a professional third party), and a *beneficiary* (a charity). It also has an *income beneficiary*, which can be you, your spouse, etc.

Funding the trust. Once you establish the trust, you "fund" it with "property." After the initial contribution, you can continue to add to it anytime you desire. You can even leave property through your will or trust. The trust can be funded with property in the form of appreciated assets, such as real estate or stock.

Benefits of the trust. First, for your contribution, you receive a *federal income tax deduction.* The amount of that deduction is based on the "present value" of the interest income you will receive from the trust. (Present value refers to the economic value today of the stream of income you will receive in the future.) The write-off also takes into consideration such factors as the age of the income beneficiaries (to determine how long you might receive the income), current interest rates (to calculate present value of the income stream), your adjusted gross income (to determine the amount of charitable write-off to which you are entitled), type of property (cash and real estate, for example, are treated differently), and the interest rate you will be receiving over the years. It is a complicated calculation for which I use a sophisticated computer program.

The second benefit occurs if you contribute appreciated property (stock, real estate, business interest, etc.). Since the trust is a tax-exempt entity, trust property in most cases can be sold with *no capital gains tax.* Be aware that a charitable contribution of appreciated property is a tax preference item that can create an alternative minimum tax (AMT) liability in a few situations. Check with your CPA to learn any AMT ramifications.

Third, if you serve as your own trustee, *you* control how the money is invested. Generally speaking, you can choose between stocks, bonds, mutual funds or annuities. As with any investment, it should be consistent with your financial goals, risk tolerance, years to retirement and the interest of the charitable beneficiary.

Fourth, you will *receive income* from the trust.

- To the extent that it is available, you may receive a fixed percentage of the trust assets. You have a choice in how you want to receive it—annually, semiannually, quarterly or, sometimes, monthly.
- The amount of income you receive depends on the size of the trust in addition to how you've invested your assets.
- Depending on the type of trust, you can receive only income (no principal), or a payout of both interest and principal to the extent principal is needed to reach the income rate (percentage) that you have chosen.

Fifth, upon the death of the last income beneficiary (usually you and your spouse), the *proceeds go to the charity* or charities of your choice. But they must be legitimate charities. In addition, many people choose to set up a *family foundation*. This permits their children to dispense the funds to charities over the years.

Protection for your children

The one concern I always hear is, "If I receive the income until both my wife (husband) and I die, and then the principal goes to a charity, then what's in it for my kids?" That's no problem. All we need to do is establish what we call a "wealth replacement trust." You'll recognize it as a variation of the irrevocable life insurance trust discussed earlier.

You take some of the tax benefits (remember, you get a write-off for the contribution) and/or some of the cash flow and gift it to the insurance trust. The trustee will then purchase a life insurance policy (such as a second-to-die) in the trust for the benefit of the children. If structured properly, this does several things: 1) It removes the proceeds of your life insurance from your estate; 2) it ensures that your children will receive their rightful inheritance; and 3) it protects those values from a lawsuit.

The trust in action

So the bottom line is this: You can contribute as much or as little as you want; the money is protected from lawsuits; it is free from estate taxes; you can include and exclude anyone you want; you can turn the income stream on and off as you want; and you receive a tax deduction for the contribution.

Helen and Larry Peterson, ages 62 and 61 respectively, owned real estate that they purchased years ago for $120,000. The value had appreciated to $1 million. Mr. Peterson was planning to retire within two years. He wanted to sell the real estate and invest the proceeds in something that would provide some income. The problem was that he and his heirs would have had to pay significant taxes on that money: income tax at sale; estate tax at death.

Sales Price	$1,000,000
Cost Basis	120,000
Gross Profit	$880,000
Income Taxes	299,200
Net Profit	$700,800
Estate Taxes	385,440
Net to Heirs	$315,360

Almost 70 percent of the value of the property would have been lost to income and estate taxes! (This calculation assumes current federal, capital gains, and average state income tax rates.) This means if the Petersons had *sold* the property, *paid* the capital gains tax, reinvested the money, *spent* the income, and then *died*, their heirs would have received only $315,360 of the $1 million!

This really concerned Mr. Peterson. He had visions of leaving a large sum to his children, not to Uncle Sam. He was already getting hit badly enough by taxes and didn't want to make it worse. So let's look at how he improved his situation.

Instead of selling the property outright, the Petersons established a CRUT and donated the property to it. Exhibit 8 illustrates how this worked. Let's go through it step by step. Because your situation will be different from the Petersons, we are not going to include any AMT ramifications in our calculations.

Step 1. The Petersons contributed their $1 million piece of property to their charitable remainder trust, which then sold it.

Step 2. They received a tax deduction of $275,620, which resulted in an income tax savings of $125,683.

Step 3. They took $11,138 and funded the first year's life insurance premium in a wealth replacement trust.

Step 4. The $1 million from the sale of the property was invested in bonds that averaged 7 percent per year income. After income taxes, they should receive a total of $819,812 over their life expectancy.

Step 5. They are taking part of that income each year for the next nine years to fund the life insurance trust. That amount should total $175,077, based on current projections.

Step 6. Upon their deaths, their family foundation should receive $1,528,784, based on their current life expectancy and current projections.

Step 7. Additionally, their heirs (children) will receive $1 million from the insurance trust, estate and income tax-free.

Let's compare two alternatives:

Alternative 1. The Petersons *sell the property* as they would normally. They pay the capital gains taxes, and reinvest it at 5 percent tax-free. At their deaths, the money, after estate taxes, goes to their kids.

Alternative 2. The Petersons *contribute the property* to their CRUT, which sells it and reinvests the proceeds at 7 percent, taxable. They receive the income and use part of that to purchase a life insurance policy in a wealth replacement trust. At the second death, the insurance proceeds go to their children, while the balance of the CRUT goes to their family foundation.

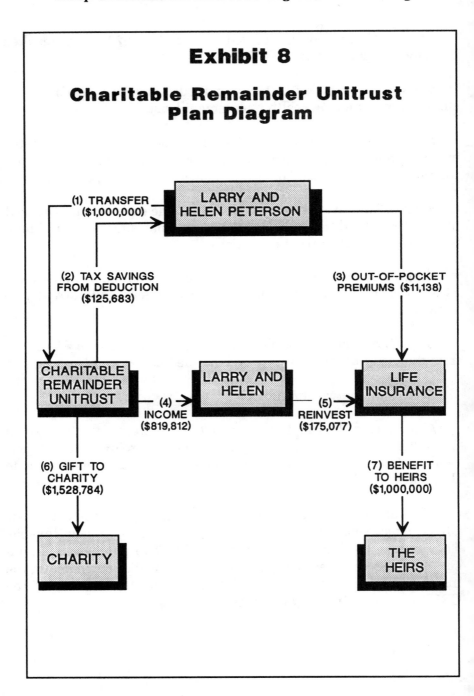

Exhibit 8

Charitable Remainder Unitrust Plan Diagram

(1) TRANSFER ($1,000,000)

LARRY AND HELEN PETERSON

(2) TAX SAVINGS FROM DEDUCTION ($125,683)

(3) OUT-OF-POCKET PREMIUMS ($11,138)

CHARITABLE REMAINDER UNITRUST

LARRY AND HELEN

LIFE INSURANCE

(4) INCOME ($819,812)

(5) REINVEST ($175,077)

(6) GIFT TO CHARITY ($1,528,784)

(7) BENEFIT TO HEIRS ($1,000,000)

CHARITY

THE HEIRS

	1. Without CRUT	2. Using CRUT
Contributions		
Market Value	$1,000,000	$1,000,000
Savings from Tax Deduction	- 0 -	125,683
Capital Gains Tax on Sale	299,200	- 0 -
Net to Invest	$700,800	$1,125,683
Cash Flow		
Income During Life	$825,637	$945,495
Less: Insurance Premiums	- 0 -	186,207
Net Spendable Income	$825,637	$759,288
Estate for Heirs		
Gross Value of Estate	$700,800	- 0 -
Plus: Life Insurance	- 0 -	$1,000,000
Less: Estate Taxes	385,440	- 0 -
Net Estate for Heirs	$315,360	$1,000,000
Summary of Benefits		
Net Income	$825,637	$759,288
Estate for Heirs	315,360	1,000,000
Amount to Charity	- 0 -	1,528,784
Total Benefit	**$1,140,997**	**$3,288,072**

You can see the leverage the Petersons could achieve with a properly structured charitable unitrust. If they had needed more income, they could have just reduced the amount of life insurance. If they didn't need all the income, they could have increased the life insurance. Whatever their needs, the flexibility is tremendous. It provides income for them, a substantial estate (free from income and estate taxes) for their children, and a considerable benefit for their favorite charities.

There are many other instances where a charitable trust can be used to reduce capital gains exposure. You might have a business you wish to sell in which you have a very low cost basis. Possibly you have a tremendous profit in a stock but don't want to sell it because of the capital gains. There are various situations where the proper use of a charitable remainder unitrust can be extremely beneficial to all the parties. Selling your business/farm/professional practice is covered in Chapter 28.

Charitable trusts as retirement plans

Many of my professional and business clients complain about their retirement plans. As a rule, there are three problems. First, the pension plan is overfunded, meaning that no additional contributions can be made. Second, so much has to be contributed for the employees that the owner receives little actual benefit. And third, the owner is penalized with the "success tax" discussed earlier in the book.

Benefits

One of the alternatives you might consider is the use of a CRUT as a retirement plan, which offers many benefits.

- You can make contributions for yourself and not include any other person.
- There are no mandated contributions; you can contribute as much or as little as you wish.
- There are no penalties for early withdrawal or requirements that you start receiving income.
- You can choose among many investment options that could allow you to receive tax-free income upon your retirement.
- You can provide a lifetime income for yourself and your spouse.
- Generally, you receive a partial tax deduction for your contribution.
- You can leave money to your children, estate tax-free, through a wealth replacement trust.
- You can leave substantial dollars to your favorite charity or charities.
- The funds in the trust are protected from lawsuits. Of course, when you start receiving income, that portion is not protected.

- There is no "success" penalty for excess accumulations or distributions.

Conclusion

This example is not designed to be an in-depth comparison of the benefits of a CRUT and a qualified retirement plan. With the latter, there are many factors involved. However, many physicians and executives are using CRUTs to supplement their qualified plan.

While in some respects, a qualified retirement plan makes sense because of the 100-percent write-off, there is a trade-off. You are subject to early withdrawal penalties and forced distributions; you must include all employees; you have outrageous administrative expenses; you have little control; and you can get penalized for superior performance.

With the CRUT, while the write-off is smaller, you can leave more to your favorite charities, you can maintain control over the trust, you can receive all the benefits yourself, you can include whomever you desire, and, properly structured, your heirs will receive their inheritance estate tax-free.

More of my clients agree that the charitable remainder unitrust should play an important part in their overall planning. They feel that with the wealth replacement trust, the benefits are immense. And slowly but surely, the more knowledgeable accountants and attorneys are beginning to see that it's not a tax-avoidance scheme, but a legitimate plan that provides unique benefits for their clients. Once they understand what a great planning tool it is, they appreciate it even more.

Twenty

How Can I Avoid Losing Up To 80 Percent of My Retirement Plan?

There are several taxes we as Americans consider especially unfair. Among those, in my opinion, is the excise tax on pension plans—what I call a "success tax."

Face it. Congress doesn't like people with money (except themselves). So besides the other taxes you are facing, the government penalizes you for having a successful retirement plan.

You know, by this point, that you pay income taxes on the money you earn, and estate taxes on the money you pass in excess of your exemption. What you might not know, however, is that there is an additional tax on retirement plans that either accumulate "too much money" or distribute "too much money." I put quotation marks around those three words because the definition has been established by your Congress.

The rules

Excess distributions. You may be subject to a 15-percent excess distribution penalty if you withdraw the greater of $150,000 or $112,500 indexed for inflation ($144,551 in 1993) from your retirement account. However, if you take your retirement in a lump sum and qualify for averaging, that amount increases to $750,000.

Excess accumulations. Leaving your money in your retirement plan is no answer, because there is a 15-percent excess accumulation penalty if you die with over the $150,000 or $112,500 ($144,551 in 1993). This amount is in *addition* to any estate taxes and not reduced by the unified credit or deductions.

The taxes

Robert Armond, a widower, had a gross estate of $3.8 million, including a $2 million pension. Upon his death, his children inherited everything. They were shocked when they found out that they would only keep $467,339 of his $2 million pension!

His $2 million pension was reduced as follows (numbers have been rounded):

Gross Pension		**$2,000,000**
Less: Excise Tax	$37,573	
Less: Estate Taxes	$1,024,335	
Less: Income Taxes	$370,753	
Total Taxes		$1,532,661
Net to Children		**$467,339**

Your particular figures depend on many factors, such as age (and life expectancy), marital status, estate and income tax brackets, current interest rates, etc. It's another one of those calculations best performed by a computer.

Grandfathering

There was a grandfather election available in 1986 that would have given you a break. If the amounts in your plans totaled at least $562,500, only the growth after that date would be subject to the excise tax. However, you had to make the election on your 1987 or 1988 income tax return with Form 5239.

Protection

Once again, you are penalized by your government for being a responsible, successful person. Are there any solutions? A few, but none are very attractive.

You can leave your money in your plan, and continue to contribute the maximum. After all, it is for your retirement, not your children's, and you will at least enjoy the benefits. However, that means you face the maximum liability. (By the way, no real problems are faced until the death of both you and your spouse, since excise and estate taxes aren't due until the death of the second spouse, and your surviving spouse can roll over your retirement plan into his or her own IRA rollover, avoiding income taxes until withdrawn.)

Second, you can withdraw money periodically and gift it to your children. Remember, you and your spouse can each make annual $10,000 gifts to any person or persons you want. You would have to pay income taxes on the withdrawals, but that would avoid the income and excise tax (assuming those withdrawals didn't run into the "excess distribution" penalty).

Third, you can make withdrawals and purchase a life insurance policy. This can be structured to avoid income and estate taxes. Therefore, you only have to pay income taxes on the money you withdraw from your pension. By following the instructions in Chapter 16, you can convert money that would be subject to all taxes and avoid everything but current income taxes on the withdrawal.

Fourth, you could consider another "nonqualified" retirement plan, such as a charitable remainder trust. This would allow you to put aside money for you, without including any other employees. This was described in the previous chapter.

Conclusion

This tax, or a variation of it, is due on all retirement distributions, which includes qualified plans and IRAs. Because of the complexity of this situation, I recommend you consult with a CPA, tax attorney and financial planner. Together, they should be able to help you reduce the burden of the success tax.

Twenty-One

What Are Some More Advanced Methods of Reducing Taxes?

To this point, we have covered most of the more common ways to reduce your estate taxes. Though it is not my intent to cover every possible strategy, I would like to touch on some advanced methods that I use to help my clients reduce their taxes. These can be helpful if your estate exceeds $600,000 if you are single, or $1.2 million if you are married.

An initial word of caution. These techniques aren't for everyone. They apply in certain situations only. Don't do any planning without the assistance of a competent estate planner and attorney.

Family limited partnerships

In Chapter 27, Attorney Kelly Burke discusses how to use family limited partnerships (FLPs) to reduce your liability exposure. I would like to talk about how to use them to reduce your income taxes and estate taxes.

FLPs consist of two classes of partners: general partners and limited partners. The general partners run the partnership, assume the liability exposure, and get paid a salary for their work. The limited partners have no exposure, make no decisions, receive no salary, but do receive their share of the income (or losses.)

Ownership is split between the classes. Generally, the bulk of the ownership is vested with the limited partner(s), for the reasons we shall see shortly. However, regardless of his or her percentage of ownership, the general partner always maintains control.

173

Joanne and Rodney Towson have an estate valued at $4 million. The bulk of it consists of timberland that produces erratic income, but is consistent in its value. They would like to reduce their estate and income taxes, but would still like to retain control.

Although the details may vary, this is a common problem and concern. The family limited partnership can help. Let's look at the steps.

1. An FLP is established with you as the general partner and your spouse and/or children as limited partners. You may own any percentage you want. However, whatever you give to your children as limited partners is considered a gift. Let's assume you hold a 1-percent general partnership interest, your spouse's living trust has a 98-percent limited partnership interest, and your children's trust owns a 1-percent limited partnership interest.

2. Your partnership agreement sets forth the terms and conditions. The agreement would provide, for example, that: the general partner has all control and management rights; the general partner will determine the income distributions—although all distributions will be made on a pro-rata basis; the limited partners shall have no rights other than income distributions; the limited partners have no right to force liquidation or demand distribution; etc. An attorney can structure it to meet your needs, state statutes, and IRS regulations.

3. You then transfer your property into the partnership. At this point, your gift is minimal, since you are only giving 1 percent to your children.

4. You would then, over time, transfer limited partnership interests from your spouse to your children. The gift value of your transfers would be discounted to reflect that those properties either lack marketability or consist of a minority interest. The fact that the limited partners' interest is restricted reduces the value of those interests.

This unique vehicle has some very real advantages:

Income tax savings. The fact that income is distributed on a pro-rata basis means that the more you transfer to your children in limited partnership interests, the more income they receive. This helps reduce your income tax burden by transferring it to them.

Estate tax savings. Again, you are reducing your estate taxes by transferring ownership in your property to your children.

Liability protection. As you will see in Chapter 27, you can be afforded some very real asset protection in a properly structured FLP.

Complete control. No matter how small your general partnership ownership, you still maintain control.

In the Towson case, it was recommended that they establish the Towson Family Limited Partnership. The partnership consisted of a 1-percent general partnership share owned by Rodney and Joanne, a 45-percent limited partnership interest owned by Joanne's living trust, a 45-percent limited partnership interest owned by Rodney's living trust, and a 9-percent limited partnership interest owned by their four children. They transferred their $3 million in timberland into the trust. Since they didn't need the income, and wanted to reduce their estate, they decided to make annual gifts to their children. With four children and spouses, they can each gift $80,000, or a total of $160,000 annually. But, based on their situation, they receive a lack of marketability discount of 35 percent. That means that they can give a total of $246,154 annually and still fall within their annual gifts. This will have the effect of reducing their income taxes, as their children receive more of the income, and reducing their estate taxes, since more and more of the assets go to the children. Nevertheless, they will always maintain control.

Family limited partnerships, of course, are not without their disadvantages:

Expense. FLPs are among the most costly estate planning technique. They can range from $5,000 to $15,000 to set up.

Complexity. As you can tell from our discussion, these are not simple devices. They have to be handled properly and meet all state and IRS regulations.

Qualified advice. To pull this together, you must seek qualified advice. Otherwise, all your efforts will be for naught.

We have here a unique planning tool that, under the right circumstances, can be an unbelievably terrific planning tool. Just make sure you use it wisely with proper counsel.

Generation skipping

I work with many older citizens who want to provide for their grandchildren. By doing so, they can accomplish three things. First, they can help secure the financial future of their grandchildren. Second, by giving away assets, they can reduce their own estates. Third, if their children are going to have an estate tax problem, then by skipping them and leaving assets directly to their grandchildren, they can save estate taxes at their children's death. Otherwise, by the time the grandchildren receive it, it could be whittled down to a fraction of its former value. As a result, the incentive for skipping generations is great.

Unfortunately, the government also realized the benefit, and, in its normal fashion, has set up a handful of restrictive rules to deter its use.

- A generation skipping tax of 55 percent is charged on all transfers to a person or persons two or more generations below (younger) than the transferor.
- This tax is in addition to any estate or gift taxes that are incurred.
- The generation skipping tax rate is the maximum estate tax rate in effect at the time (currently 55 percent).

However, all is not lost. There are some generation skipping provisions.

- Every person may exempt $1 million for generation skipping tax purposes.
- The transfers may occur one of three ways: as a distribution (such as from a trust); upon death; or as a gift.
- The transferor may exempt transfers under his $10,000 annual exclusion except, as a rule, for transfers into a trust.

These rules have drastically reduced the effectiveness of generation skipping. The fact that, if you want to distribute more than $1 million to your grandchildren at your death, you can actually pay more in taxes (caused by the combination of the generation skipping tax and the estate tax) than the gift itself reduces your incentive to generation skip, which is exactly what the government wants.

The most confusing part to some is that the generation skipping exemption is not in addition to your $600,000 exemption, it is part of it. So, while it doesn't save a whole lot of money at your death, the big advantage is that it, and the growth, are not taxed at your child's death.

Creating wealth with generation skipping

Since a $1 million exemption can ordinarily only shelter a $1 million transfer, those individuals with large estates who would like to leave more property to their grandchildren and great-grandchildren are limited. If they do take advantage of the exemption, the balance of their estate will still be heavily taxed. However, there is one way to maximize that exemption, and that is with life insurance in an irrevocable trust.

With life insurance, instead of creating only $1 million for your grandchildren, you can create many times that. In the Masons' example, we saw how they could create $600,000 from a $100,000 investment. Imagine what they could have done if they had a larger estate and used their $1 million exemption to purchase an insurance policy for the benefit of their grandchildren! They could have created over *$6 million estate and income tax-free* besides substantially reducing the size of their estate. The possibilities are endless, and the dollars created enormous.

GRITS, GRATS and GRUTS

No, these aren't menu choices at a Southern restaurant. They are yet additional special types of trusts to help reduce your estate by removing property but allowing you continued enjoyment. They all involve transferring property into an irrevocable trust, and then receiving benefit from that property for the rest of their lives. The transfer into the trust represents a gift, valued at a discounted rate. However, because the recipients (beneficiaries of the trust) don't have use of that gift, it does not qualify under the $10,000 exclusion. Upon death of the grantor, assuming he or she lives the required number of years, the property is excluded from his or her estate.

GRITS. Prior to a tax-law change in 1990, GRITS (Grantor Retained Income Trust) were a very popular estate planning tool. The way they worked is that a parent, for example, put real estate into a special trust for the benefit of her children. At the end of a certain period of time, say 10 years, the trust terminated and the property went to the children. Meanwhile, the parent received the income.

The advantage was that the real estate put into the trust was valued at a reduced amount that was effectively the present value of a future gift. Therefore, the gift to the child was only a fraction of the value. Additionally, if the parent lived longer than the term of the trust, there would be no estate taxes due on the real estate when it passed to the children.

But, like so many wonderful estate planning methods, this one, too, bit the dust. The law provides now that for everything other than "qualified interests" (which we will discuss shortly), the retained interest will have a value of zero. That means that the entire amount contributed to the trust will be a taxable gift.

There are, however, two primary exceptions under which the original rules will apply: first, if the beneficiaries are not family members; and second, if the property transferred is a personal residence.

The Personal Residence GRIT shouldn't be overlooked. If the parent transfers her home into the trust, the gift is at reduced value, just like under the old rules. Upon termination of the trust, the home belongs to the children, estate and gift tax free, although the parent may continue to live in it. If she does, however, she must pay rent to the trust. But, again, she has removed the value of her home from her estate.

GRATS. One of the "qualified interests" stated previously is the *grantor retained annuity trust*. In this case, the parent would retain the right to received fixed annuity payments for that 10-year (or predetermined) period. At the end of that period, the parent would receive no further benefits from the trust and the property would be distributed to the children. Like the GRIT, if the parent outlives the term of the trust, no estate taxes would be due at her death.

GRUTS. The other "qualified interest" is the *grantor retained unitrust*. What differentiates this from a GRAT is that the parent has the right to receive an income based on a percentage of the fair market value of the property transferred. Therefore, while the payments under a GRAT will remain constant, under a GRUT they will vary. This can prove to be an advantage as the value of the assets increase over time. On the other hand, the income can also decrease.

Private annuity

Don't confuse private annuities with products sold by insurance company. A private annuity is a contract between two parties:

1. The transferor, who transfers ownership of assets to a third party.
2. The transferee, who receives the assets, and promises to make payments to the transferor for the remainder of his (the transferor's) life, or that of the transferor and his or her spouse.

John and Mary Berry own shares of a publicly held corporation. The stock, which provides income, has a low cost basis, and has appreciated greatly. If they pass the stock to their children upon their deaths, it will result in substantial capital gains. If they gift it to them, it will: 1) keep their low cost basis, and 2) mean that they may no longer receive the income.

A private annuity may be just the thing for the Berrys. They would transfer the stock to their children in return for a promise of the children to pay them an income for the rest of their lives. The income they receive is based upon an annuity factor, which is the fair market value divided by a factor based on the Berry's ages and current interest rates. There would be several advantages to the Berrys.

- The stock would be out of their estate, thus saving substantial estate taxes.
- They would receive an income for the rest of their lives.
- After the Berrys' death, the cost basis of the children would be the total annuity payments they made to their parents.
- The transfer to their children would not result in gift taxes.

- Only part of the income would be subject to income taxes. The balance would be considered a "return of principal," and thus not subject to income taxes.

However, there are some disadvantages.

- The obligation of the children to make the payments cannot be secured by the asset transferred or any other asset.
- If the parents live too long, the children may end up making payments longer than expected, thus increasing the size of their parent's estate.

Conclusion

There are some very unique planning opportunities still available for the right situations. These can help significantly reduce your estate tax exposure. But again, you need competent financial and legal advice to make these work. Make sure you seek it out.

Twenty-Two

How Will I be Affected if the Exemption is Reduced?

There have been rumblings in Congress since 1992 about reducing the exemption from $600,000 to $200,000 or $300,000. This direct attack on conscientious, prudent, hard-working people is unwarranted. The result would be devastating to the average American.

Personally, I am sick and tired of Congress treating hard-working citizens like they are a blight on society. Not a day goes by that I don't speak with somebody who is scared to death about what is happening to their security.

What gives Congress the right to think that they can confiscate everything you have worked for? While your representatives talk about supporting middle Americans, they do everything in their power to destroy you.

I don't think that our representatives in Congress care one bit about hard-working people. Instead, they see you as a big dollar sign; a bottomless pit to support their waste and fraud. I don't think that they care that your taxes keep going up and you get less for your money. And I don't think that they want you to pass what you've worked for to your family. They want it all!

The ramifications

The following table gives you a rough idea of how your estate taxes will be affected when they change the law. You can see that you don't have to be rich to get soaked. In fact, this would affect smaller estate more than larger estates, on a percentage basis. If Congress has it way, it won't be the "rich" who get socked with estate taxes...it'll be the average American.

Current Estate Size	$600,000 Exemption	$500,000 Exemption	$400,000 Exemption	$300,000 Exemption	$200,000 Exemption
$300,000	0	0	0	0	33,000
400,000	0	0	0	34,000	67,000
500,000	0	0	34,000	68,000	101,000
600,000	0	37,000	71,000	105,000	138,000
1,000,000	153,000	190,000	224,000	258,000	291,000
3,000,000	1,098,000	1,135,000	1,169,000	1,203,000	1,236,000

What is "rich"?

The problem arises when you try to define who is rich under the "soak the rich" philosophy that is so prevalent today. Currently, a $600,000 exemption protects the majority of citizens of this country from paying estate taxes. However, when you reduce the exemption to $200,000, it's a far different story. A home in certain parts of the country, a farm in the Midwest, timberland in the South, land in the West, a life insurance policy, a business...all these can easily push you above the $200,000 threshold. Does that make you rich? I don't think so. But your government does.

Understand what a reduction in the unified credit will do to what you have worked your lifetime to accumulate. Think about how it will affect you, your parents and your children. It's not a pretty picture.

Protection

You've got two choices. You can do something now, while the exemption is still $600,000, or you can wait until it changes. Let's look at some steps you can take, in order of my recommended use.

Take advantage of both exemptions. We previously discussed the use of a trust to capture both spouse's exemption. By doing this, you can double your exemption. Under current law, utilizing both $600,000 exemptions would protect up to $1.2 million. If the exemption is reduced to $200,000, using both exemptions would protect $400,000.

Remove your life insurance. Remember from our earlier discussion, life insurance is part of your taxable estate. By having your life insurance owned either by your children or an irrevocable trust, it is not subject to estate taxes at your death. If you change ownership of your life insurance within three years of your death, it still remains part of your taxable estate.

Maximize gifting. You can make $10,000 gifts to any person you desire. By taking advantage of these gifts to children and grand-children, you can substantially reduce your taxable estate.

Use your $600,000 exemption today. You have the option of using your $600,000 while you're alive or after your dead. If you want to make sure you won't lose if they reduce the exemption, use it today. You can do that by giving assets directly to your children or putting it in an irrevocable trust. By doing that now, you will not only remove $600,000 from your estate, but you will remove the growth as well.

Take advantage of advanced methods. In the previous chapter, I spoke about GRITS, GRATS, GRUTS, charitable trusts, family limited partnerships, and private annuities. Any of these techniques will help you reduce estate taxes.

Conclusion

We don't know when Congress is going to drop the bomb. All we know is that it is on its way. Don't wait to take advantage of these methods. If you postpone protecting your estate until the government acts, it will be too late.

Part IV

Protection During Your Lifetime

Twenty-Three

How Can I Protect Myself if I Become Disabled?

"Disability" is a word that scares many people. And it should. At most ages, your chances of becoming disabled are many times greater than your chances of dying. Yet while many people have made some type of plan in case of their premature death, few have taken action to protect themselves and their families in the event of their disability.

This chapter addresses both aspects of disability: the disability that keeps you from working and earning a living, and the disability that keeps you from making financial decisions.

Disability from work

If you became disabled today, could you support yourself and your family? Would you have sufficient income to meet your everyday expenses? Could you make your mortgage, car and credit card payments? Could you buy food, clothing and medical supplies? If not, then you need to look carefully at disability insurance.

A disability occurs as the result of an accident or sickness that keeps you from earning an income. If you work for the government, or a corporation, or a generous employer, then you probably have insurance to cover you in this event. If you don't, you may want to give it a look.

Disability insurance pays you a monthly income when you are unable to work. When talking about disability insurance, there are some decisions you need to make and some factors you need to consider.

Waiting period is the number of days until your disability benefits begin. Obviously, the shorter the waiting period, the higher the premium.

Benefit period is the number of years for which you will receive benefits. It can range anywhere from two years to your lifetime. The longer the benefit period, the higher the premium.

Benefit amount is the monthly income you will be paid by the insurance company. This is a percentage of your income, usually limited to 60 percent.

Premium payor is the party paying the premium. If you have a corporation, then that entity can pay and deduct the premium. However, the benefits are taxable when you receive them. On the other hand, if you pay the benefits yourself, they are not tax-deductible, but neither are the benefits income-taxable when you receive them.

Your job description will have a large bearing on the premium. Obviously, if you work at a hazardous waste site, your premiums will be higher than if you work in an office.

The **definition of disability** determines when the insurance company considers you disabled. Much of this depends on your job. A professional (such as a physician), can receive benefits if he or she is unable to continue the duties of his or her particular specialty. An unskilled worker, on the other hand, will receive benefits as long as he is unable to perform any job for which he is suited.

Continuation of coverage is your right to maintain the coverage and current premium. You should look for a policy that is guaranteed renewable and noncancelable.

Mental incapacity

Beyond what we just covered, there is also another category of disability. It is the type that will not only render you incapable of working but will also make you incapable of making financial decisions. This is the area that relates to estate planning.

Jack Johnson and his wife Ruth had a difficult life. They had overcome many financial and medical problems. To make matters worse, one day Jack was hit by a car while jogging and ended up in a coma. The bulk of their property was in joint tenancy. Ruth, shaken by the entire experience, was nevertheless ready to carry on with the family's finances. However, she ran into some problems.

Jack began receiving a monthly disability check. Ruth didn't know how she should handle depositing the checks since they were payable to her husband.

The Johnsons had a brokerage account with a local firm. One day, Ruth needed money and called the broker to sell some stock. If the broker had known that Jack was mentally disabled, he would not have executed the trade, because joint accounts require the authority of both parties. Even if he had done what she wanted, the check would have been payable to Mr. and Mrs. Johnson. She was not sure whether to tell the broker the truth.

She wanted to sell their home, which was owned jointly. She knew she couldn't do this without his signature.

Now we all realize that people sign their spouse's names on checks every day of the week. But it is against the law. Banks can't accept forgeries, even by a spouse. And I know stockbrokers transact business in joint accounts after speaking with only one party. But that's not supposed to happen either. The fact is that Mrs. Johnson's hands were tied financially. She ran into a roadblock at every turn.

What we have is a string of problems for which most people don't plan, but more than a few experience. In fact, we don't think we have a problem until we have a problem. And as long as both Mr. and Mrs. Johnson were functioning normally, they didn't have a problem. But Jack became disabled, so all of a sudden, they did have a problem, and a big one at that.

Living probate

We talked about death probate earlier. Living probate, on the other hand, is a process in which a person is declared mentally incompetent and a guardian is appointed. Basically, it entails the embarrassing situation of having to lay before the probate court the details concerning the person claimed to be incapacitated. Then, after the necessary doctor's statements, testimony, etc., the court appoints a guardian.

Groucho Marx

We all know who Groucho Marx was—a great comedian. As Groucho got older, he became more and more unable to make decisions. His health, like that of many older people, deteriorated. At the time, he had a live-in girlfriend, Erin Fleming. Erin felt that Groucho could no longer make his own decisions, so she petitioned the court to have him declared mentally incompetent. In order to do this, Groucho had to go through living probate.

In this case, the court appointed Erin as guardian and the Bank of America as custodian of the funds. This went on for a while, but Erin didn't like it; she didn't want the bank involved. So she petitioned the court again, this time to be named sole custodian. There was, however, considerable negative reaction. The bank trustees didn't like it and thought that their bank should be named sole custodian. Groucho's family came out of the woodwork and decided that one of them should be named custodian.

You probably remember what happened next. It was in all the newspapers and on television. Groucho went through a long, humiliating proceeding during which witnesses, friends, enemies and anyone else who had anything to say took the stand and testified. All kinds of bad stuff came out. Groucho just sat in his wheelchair the entire time and listened, tears rolling down his cheeks, unable to contribute. It was a sad situation.

After a lengthy proceeding, Groucho's grandson was named custodian. Shortly thereafter, Groucho Marx died. A sad ending to a great life. But it wasn't over. Groucho's estate had to go through more—his will had to be probated!

Who made all the money from this fiasco? Three guesses. Even with all the legal advice that Groucho received (or should I say "because of all the legal advice"), he wasn't spared this humiliation and expense.

The Groucho Marx story is a famous case because of his status as a celebrity. After hearing that story, many people say, "I'm not rich and famous like Groucho; this could never happen to me." It certainly could. Read on.

Blanche Hardy's husband, Franklin, was a logger for a timber company. While cutting timber one day, a tree "kicked-back" and knocked Franklin out. In fact, the doctors didn't expect him to live.

After a week, however, the doctor said to Blanche, "The good news is your husband is going to live; the bad news is he will have the mind of a 3-year-old." She was devastated. But she loved him and wanted to spend every hour she could with him at the hospital. She was determined to see it through.

Enter the insurance company. The workers' compensation carrier was paying Franklin a monthly benefit. They were afraid that he might die, resulting in a large death claim. They decided it would be better if Franklin was transferred to a town across the state that had a large medical complex. That way, in the event that he needed special care, he would be close to good facilities. His wife didn't agree. She and Franklin had grown up in their small town and felt comfortable there with all their friends and relatives. She didn't want to pick up and move to a strange location, even if the medical care was superior.

The insurance company didn't like that. They went to Franklin's brother in this other town and offered him a lump sum of money plus a monthly stipend if he would petition for guardianship of his brother. Each side had its own attorneys. They went through all the legalities: interrogatories, depositions, briefs, etc. The Saturday evening before the Monday when the hearing was scheduled, Blanche dropped dead of a heart attack! Her doctor said she had been in perfect health and didn't have any heart problems. He surmised that the stress killed her.

This is but one of many tragic stories played out across this country every day. Most people feel comfortable in thinking that nothing bad will ever happen. Well, bad things do happen. Read on.

Mildred and Paul Hansen lived a happy and secure life. Mr. Hansen was a successful businessman and provided his family with a comfortable lifestyle. They had two children, who at the time were 14 and 20. One evening, Mr. and Mrs. Hansen were in a automobile accident. Mr. Hansen died immediately. Mrs. Hansen was in serious condition at the local hospital. The older child came home from college to care for his sister. The only problem was the children didn't have any money. Their father's assets were tied up in his estate. The mother was incapable of doing anything with her money because of her medical condition. They didn't even have money to pay for food. Luckily, however, their aunts and uncles helped out. The cemetery wanted cash for the burial plot for their father. Again, they didn't have any funds. Mortgage payments had to be paid. Utilities. Car payments. Again, their aunts and uncles chipped in and made the necessary payments. When Mildred was released from the hospital, she repaid her brothers and sisters.

You can see that this isn't one of those disaster stories where someone got kicked out of his home. Nobody starved for lack of food. The electricity wasn't turned off. But it did create unnecessary hardship. The family just didn't plan because they never dreamed that it would happen to them. Remember, we don't think we have a problem until we have a problem. But you can bet they are planning now. Since that episode, Mrs. Hansen has structured her entire estate so this can't happen again. The children, now grown, realize what must be done to avoid these types of problems. They don't want to put their children through what they went through.

Darla and Sam Estes had been married over 45 years when Sam suffered a major stroke and ended up in a nursing home. Since all the property had been in Sam's name, Darla had to go through living probate to be appointed his guardian. Although an unpleasant experience, it was a piece of cake compared with what came next. Since she was guardian of his property, it could be used only for his benefit, even though she needed support. The court told her she couldn't use it for taxes. She couldn't use it for food. She couldn't use it for her benefit at all. She was in a terrible fix. Her attorney could not convince the probate court that she should receive some money. They kept coming back to the fact that she was guardian over his property, and as such, it could only be used for him.

This was certainly not acceptable to her, so she hired another attorney. This one took a different tact: he threatened the court that Darla would divorce Sam. According to the rules of their state, she would then be able to get half his money. Although the thought distressed Darla, she realized this was her only hope. Thankfully, that wasn't necessary. The court gave in and became more reasonable. Nevertheless, the entire episode took a terrible financial and emotional toll on Darla.

*   *   *

Back to the Johnson case discussed earlier. As noted, Ruth had some problems. She was handcuffed financially since all their property was in joint tenancy. She met with an attorney who advised her that the best course was for her husband to be declared incompetent by the court and she appointed guardian. The attorney filed a petition before the court and alleged that Mr. Johnson was incompetent. After a period of time, the court held hearings. Mrs. Johnson's lawyer introduced affidavits by the doctors attesting to Jack's incompetence. Mrs. Johnson was appointed guardian. The court required a bond for the full amount of the estate and further required that Mrs. Johnson file a return with the court annually and account for every penny.

But that only solved part of her problem. She still wanted to sell some stock. The brokerage firm wouldn't allow it without court approval. Therefore, her lawyer again petitioned the court for a hearing on the sale of the stock. After 30 days, the hearing was held and no objections were raised. The stock could be sold with the proceeds placed in an FDIC-insured bank.

As discussed earlier, she also wanted to sell her home. Her attorney told her to go ahead and get a contract for the sale. Once obtained, the attorney again filed a petition before the court for a public hearing. Again, in 30 days the hearing was held, the contract submitted, and the sale approved. As before, the funds had to be deposited in an FDIC-insured bank.

You can see from the Johnsons' case that living probate was not an attractive proposition. It put the surviving spouse in the very difficult position of having to answer to the court, not to mention incurring additional expenses. While every state has different procedures, the methods of obtaining guardianship or conservatorship are similar. Somebody has to be appointed guardian, and only the court can do it.

Handling incapacity: Durable Power of Attorney

Many people use a power of attorney to avoid potential incapacity problems. A power of attorney permits one person to act for another. In most states, this "general" power of attorney becomes invalid upon the disability of the maker. Therefore, a "durable" power of attorney, which is valid even upon the disability of the maker, is necessary.

A power of attorney is the easiest, and most dangerous, solution to the problem of disability. The reason it is so easy is because it costs virtually nothing to draw up and is usually relatively simple to work with. You can find the necessary forms at most office supply stores. On the other hand, it contains some real and very dangerous dragons.

Some institutions might choose not to accept it. Many times a bank will refuse to accept a power of attorney. Clients have told me that many financial institutions require that you use only their forms. This can get cumbersome, especially if you are constantly moving your CDs from one bank to another.

Attorneys may not choose to accept it for a real estate closing. Most closing attorneys will require that the power contain specific language pursuant to that particular piece of property. Most powers don't contain this.

Brokerage firms may refuse the power. Again, most brokerage firms require language specific to their firm or type of holdings. Some firms accept only their own form.

An older power might not be accepted. Many financial institutions put a time limit on the validity of a power of attorney. For example, they may choose not to honor a power if it has been longer than 18 months since it was signed. You can imagine the liability of an institution or an attorney who acts on a power of attorney that, unbeknownst to him or her, had been previously revoked. You might consider having your power of attorney updated periodically, such as every 18 to 24 months.

In the wrong hands, a power of attorney is a dangerous document. If you are trying to take care of all eventualities, you must give your agent broad powers. But those same powers give that person the right to do anything he or she wants, anytime he or she wants. We have all heard of situations where a child with a power of attorney has withdrawn money from his or her parent's account, or sold stocks and bonds and pocketed the money.

A power of attorney dies when the person giving the power dies. Therefore, while it might solve some problems at the disability of Mr. Johnson, it will not be helpful after his death.

A power of attorney won't solve all problems, though it might have been helpful in the Johnsons' case. But what would have happened if they both had become disabled, or if one had died and the other had become disabled, as in the case of Mildred and Paul Hansen? The power of attorney would not have done any good. The only other solution would have been to give each of their children a power, and I don't know how comfortable they would have felt with that.

Another type of power that many attorneys recommend is a "springing" power. It does not become effective until a certain "event" occurs, such as your disability. This solves the problem of having current powers floating around among family members.

Like joint tenancy, many people use a power of attorney as an inexpensive method to avoid proper estate planning. In the right situation, a power of attorney can ease the planning process. Recognize, however, that you are giving unlimited power to your agent. And acceptance of the power is not automatic. It only has value if the institution is willing to accept it. Furthermore, since you are giving so much power, it is very possible that it could backfire. Once again, trying to save some money by planning yourself could be costly in the long run.

Living trust

Another alternative to living probate and the problems with a power of attorney is the living trust. In the trust, you name a trustee or trustees to handle your affairs. You include instructions for your own care in the case of disability. Property is titled into the trust so the trustee can perform his or her duties without difficulty. The trust lists the powers granted to the trustee. Let's revisit Mr. and Mrs. Johnson and see what might have happened with better planning.

> *Mr. Johnson began receiving his monthly disability check. Their living trust would have included a "special durable power of attorney" which would have allowed only one thing: for the trustee (Mrs. Johnson) to deposit Mr. Johnson's property into the trust. She could have used this power to deposit his checks into the trust checking account.*
>
> *They owned stocks and bonds through a local brokerage firm. Whenever Ruth needed money, she would have called her broker. The brokerage account would have already been titled in the name of the trust and the brokerage firm would have had an "affidavit of trust" outlining the applicable parts of the trust. The broker would have sold the stock and issued a check, which she would have deposited into the trust checking account.*
>
> *After a while, whenever Ruth needed to sell property, she could have done it as trustee. The closing attorney would have wanted proof she was the trustee and further proof that Jack was disabled. She would have presented the applicable parts of the trust along with a letter from her physician.*

Conclusion

You can see the difference between the two scenarios. One of the advantages of a living trust over a simple power of attorney is that the trust has limitations on the powers of the trustee, whereas a power of attorney is effectively a blank check to the holder. Additionally, the trust provides contingencies in the event the trustees cannot, or will not, serve.

Again, your best course of action depends upon your particular situation. Nothing works for everybody all the time. If you are concerned about the points mentioned previously in this chapter, then a living trust might be a good solution. However, if you have absolute confidence in the person to whom you are giving power, and if you don't expect any problems, then consider a durable power of attorney as a possible solution. Just make sure you are comfortable with your choice.

Twenty-Four

How Can I Handle the Nursing Home Problem?

One area of planning that causes a tremendous amount of concern is a prolonged nursing home stay. Even if you aren't currently involved with someone facing a prolonged nursing home stay, statistically someday you may be. This is not meant to scare you—it's just fact. It is one of the most devastating problems many people will ever face. And unlike many of the concepts we have discussed that can cost you money, *this one can wipe you out financially.*

There is no doubt that the aspect that concerns most people is the cost of a prolonged stay in a nursing home. The people who are most at risk financially are those in the middle class. Whereas the government will care for the poor, and the more affluent have the cash flow and assets with which to pay, it is the group in the middle whose assets are at risk. They are too rich to be poor and too poor to be rich.

Sarah Middleton is concerned about a nursing home stay. Her health, while still fairly good, is starting to decline. Her assets total $105,000. She has checked various nursing homes and figures it will cost her $2,800 per month, which is about average. Her current income from Social Security and her late husband's retirement is $1,350.

She knows that while the cost of nursing care will continue to escalate, her income will not keep pace. What can she do? Her choices are very limited.

Obviously, she could pay the shortfall between the cost of the nursing home and her income by selling assets. Depending upon the length of her stay, however, she could very well run out of money. If that were to happen, Medicaid would pay for her nursing home stay.

- *She could buy nursing home insurance. While this can be expensive, depending on many factors, it is a viable alternative.*
- *She could give her assets away, thus qualifying her for Medicaid while preserving her estate for her children.*

Before reviewing the alternatives, examine the following graph. It shows exactly where the money for nursing homes comes from. Notice the fact that Medicare, the health insurance on which most senior citizens rely, provides virtually no benefit for nursing home care. Most payments are made either by the patient or Medicaid.

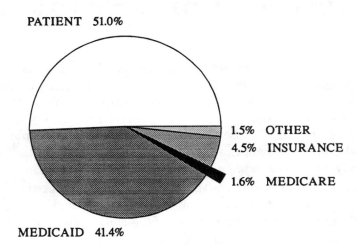

PATIENT 51.0%

1.5% OTHER

4.5% INSURANCE

1.6% MEDICARE

MEDICAID 41.4%

Let's review Mrs. Middleton's alternatives.

Pay in cash

It goes without saying that the cost of a nursing home stay is expensive and getting even more so. For Mrs. Middleton, the cost of a nursing home is $1,450 per month more than her monthly income. Assuming prices stay the same, which they won't, she could be wiped out financially in only six years.

Mrs. Middleton could take her chances and hope that: 1) she doesn't go into a nursing home; 2) if she does, her assets will be sufficient to pay; 3) if she goes in, she will not stay in too long; or 4) if she does go in, there will still be an inheritance for her children upon her death.

You can see that Mrs. Middleton has a real problem. Taking her chances leaves her with a big question mark, because she has no idea what will really happen. Like most "non-planning," it leaves everything up to chance.

Considering the statistics, which indicate that a person over the age of 65 faces a 40-percent to 50-percent chance of a nursing home stay, doing nothing is not a sensible alternative. If you have sufficient income and/or assets, you probably could afford the cost of a nursing home stay. However, if your assets are in the $50,000 to $400,000 range, you need to do some serious planning. Unfortunately, the "plan" most people choose is to do nothing.

Paying in cash means that Mrs. Middleton could deplete all her assets and leave nothing for her children. That is not what she has in mind. She and her late husband worked hard their entire lives to be comfortable and leave something for their children. The thought that all their life's efforts may go to a nursing home is not comforting.

Buy nursing home insurance

The best alternative for many people is to purchase nursing home insurance. This is a tricky one. While the idea of buying insurance to cover nursing home costs sounds good, you need to be careful. You are faced with many agents and companies trying to get premiums for coverage of questionable value, often offered by weak companies. I don't mean to insinuate that all companies offering nursing home insurance are bad. Nor am I saying that the coverage isn't worthwhile. But I have seen the results of marketing efforts by some agents and organizations offering policies to the elderly, and I don't like it.

I can't tell you how much money is wasted on various health insurance programs, most of which are totally unnecessary. So many people buy insurance that is merely a duplication of other coverage. They have not one, but two or more Medigap policies. They have intensive care coverage. Cancer coverage. Emergency room coverage. Policies that pay a stated amount per day for stays in the hospital. Physicians' coverage. Surgical coverage. So much money is spent on unnecessary coverage that it sickens me. And the people who can least afford it pay the most.

First understand that any coverage provided by Medicare and Medigap policies for a nursing home stay is very limited. You can't depend on this to be of any benefit for a nursing home, no matter what you have been told. As we saw from the graph, only 1.6 percent of nursing home expenses are paid by Medicare. This is not an alternative.

However, long-term care (nursing home) insurance *is* available, but you must be extremely careful. There are only a few companies I would consider recommending and, even then, you must be sure you know what you are getting and how much it is costing you. Let's look at the decisions you must make.

Coverage

What type of basic coverage are you going to buy? There are two areas of coverage.

1. Nursing home coverage. This will cover you while you are a patient in a nursing home only.
2. Home health care. This will cover you for nursing services in your own home.

Some companies offer these separately, and some offer them in one package. Think about your economic concerns and priorities before making any choice. Many times the home health benefit is so restrictive that it is of little benefit. If you choose nursing home coverage, make sure it covers skilled, intermediate and custodial care.

Daily benefit

How much coverage do you want? There is a wide range available here and the companies will give you a choice that falls within their minimums and maximums. Some might pay from $30 a day to $140 a day; others from $60 a day to $120 a day. Some offer different benefit amounts for nursing home and home health care. The larger your benefit, the higher your premium. Because costs will be rising in the years ahead, most companies offer some sort of inflation-adjusted benefit that will increase your daily benefit over the years.

Elimination period

How long do you want to wait before benefits begin? Most insurance companies offer a variety of choices. For example, you might want coverage that starts the first day, 21st day, 45th day or 100th day, etc. The alternatives are many. And obviously your premium will reflect this. The shorter the elimination period (which means the sooner the insurance starts paying), the higher your premium.

Benefit period

How long do you want to receive benefits? Again, you have a choice, depending on the company. For example, you may have a choice between receiving benefits for two years, three years, four years, five years or the rest of your life. The longer the benefit period, the higher the premium. Typically, we recommend a three-year benefit period because of the 30-month rule discussed in the following chapter.

The premium

The price you pay will depend upon all the factors previously discussed. The higher the benefit, the higher the premium. The shorter the elimination period, the higher the premium. The longer the benefit period, the higher the premium. The older you are, the higher the premium. What makes it so difficult is that it is impossible to know what is best for you. Nobody knows how many days, if any, you will spend in a nursing home. In most cases, the coverage chosen is a matter of affordability.

Factors you need to consider

If you decide to consider private nursing home insurance, here are some things to look for.

- The policy should be **guaranteed renewable**. That means that the company does not have the right to cancel your coverage, no matter what. The only time your coverage can end is when you: 1) stop paying the premiums or 2) exhaust your benefits.
- The policy should provide for **level premiums**. You should know, in advance, the amount of your premiums. But remember, this is health insurance. And as with your medical

insurance, the premiums can be increased. But make sure this can only be done if the company raises the premiums of everyone in your state that has the same policy.

• The policy should include **waiver of premium**. That means that if you start receiving benefits, your premiums will cease. Most policies state that the premiums will be waived after 90 days of benefit payments.

• The policy should have no limitations for **pre-existing conditions**. This means that the company should not have the right to deny coverage if you enter a nursing home due to a condition that you had previously. This is a perfect way for a company to deny coverage. Either you are approved for coverage, or turned down, nothing in between.

• Most policies exclude coverage for mental, nervous and psychotic disorders. Make sure that **Alzheimer's** and similar forms of senility or dementia are specifically covered in the policy. Don't take the agent's word. Don't accept some vague wording. It should be clear to you that this is covered.

• Do not accept a policy that is subject to **underwriting after a claim**. A few companies have tried to get cute by offering coverage subject to underwriting after a claim is submitted. That is like buying car insurance and letting the company decide if they want to cover you after you have had an accident. You don't want any problems once you submit a claim.

• There should be **no prior hospital stay** required. You don't want to get into a situation where a company will only pay if you are going into a nursing home directly from a hospital. Today, most people go directly into a nursing home without having first been in a hospital.

• Make sure the company is **A+ rated** by A.M. Best and, ideally, top-rated by another rating service. The same guidelines that we spoke about in the chapter on life insurance apply here. Don't get involved with the lower-rated companies, no matter how much the agent may try to reassure you.

- Answer **every medical question** honestly. Make sure that the agent writes down your answers. Don't leave the insurance company any room to deny your claim.

- When you receive the policy, **review it** carefully, making sure that everything you understood to be in the policy is really there. Don't take the agent's word for it. Nothing should be subject to interpretation. If it doesn't meet your approval, don't accept it. The company will refund your money if done within a set number of days.

As you can see, there is a lot to consider when dealing with nursing home insurance. But if you are careful, and follow those guidelines above, you should be able to purchase coverage to suit your needs.

Conclusion

For many people, the discussion ends here. They are either able to pay for nursing home expenses from their income and/or assets, or they can afford long-term care insurance. However, for many, the problem remains: "If I don't have the money to pay for a nursing home, and/or I can't afford or qualify for insurance, then what can I do? How can I make it through a nursing home stay while still leaving some money for my children?"

The answers to those questions are found in the following chapter.

Twenty-Five

How Can I Protect My Assets From a Nursing Home Stay?

In the previous chapter, we discussed the problems you face with a prolonged nursing home stay and reviewed two ways to pay for it: cash or insurance.

However, for many, those alternatives aren't applicable. Mrs. Middleton, for example, is not in a position to pay in cash, because her income is insufficient to cover a nursing home bill. That shortage in today's dollars is $1,450 per month. On the other hand, at her age she cannot afford nursing home insurance, either. What else can she do?

Letting the government pay

She can opt for the third alternative: letting the government pay. For some people, this is their only choice. They just don't have any money and can neither afford nor qualify for nursing home insurance. That is Mrs. Middleton's situation. Once she has used her assets to pay for her nursing home care, the government will step in.

What is Medicaid?

Medicaid is a combined federal and state program that pays the cost of a nursing home for anyone who is destitute. The issue, then, is the definition of "destitute." Since that definition is a function of a person's assets and income, we need to review specifically what Medicaid considers assets and income. This is the centerpiece of nursing home planning.

What is an asset?

According to Medicaid, basically everything you own is an asset: bank accounts, home, stocks, bonds, retirement plans, personal belongings, other investments, life insurance cash values, businesses, etc.

What is income?

Medicaid's definition of income is not unlike what yours might be: anything you receive as payment is income. This includes retirement benefits, interest, investment income, Social Security, etc. In most cases, if you have sufficient income with which to pay the nursing home bill, regardless of your asset structure, you will have to do so. If your income comes up short (as does Mrs. Middleton's), then Medicaid will make up the difference if your asset structure qualifies.

Before proceeding further, let me make a very important statement: Laws vary from state to state. Since this is a joint federal/state program, it is subject to interpretation by each individual state. Don't take any of the following rules as gospel. They can, and do, vary. Additionally, the interpretation and rules are in a constant state of flux.

What can you keep?

Medicaid doesn't require that you be "flat broke." You are permitted to keep some assets and income and still qualify for benefits. Let's take a general look. But remember, the laws are complicated and each state can and does vary.

Assets. Those assets that are not counted by Medicaid include approximately $2,000 in cash (depending on your state), a home, personal effects such as jewelry (some states have limits) and furniture, a prepaid funeral and burial account, an automobile used for transportation of the person in the nursing home, and a small amount of cash value in a life insurance policy.

Income. If you have sufficient income to pay the cost of a nursing home, you must do so. Any shortage, assuming you don't go over the asset limit above, will be paid by Medicaid. Nevertheless, you are allowed, over and above, to keep a small amount of "spending money." Be aware, however, that there are some states that disqualify you for Medicaid if your income is a certain level, even if that income is insufficient to pay your nursing home bills. This is just another tragedy of being part of the middle class.

What about the home?

This is a very interesting problem because the laws are ever changing. It has been said that the home is protected (in most states) as long as the person entering the nursing home indicates, in writing, his or her intent to return to that home. Some people have been advised to put every penny in a home, including the furnishings. I have heard of people being advised to buy the most expensive home possible and fill it with Van Gogh paintings.

This question is so difficult that even national "experts" have given incorrect information to people in various states because of the ever-evolving nature of the rules. You can even check from county to county and get conflicting answers.

Some say don't worry about the house—just sign the intent to return and it will be protected. However, under new law, states are required to recover the Medicaid expenses upon death. Therefore, protection of the home eventually terminates.

What about the stay-at-home spouse?

This is a tricky issue because you face a totally different set of problems when you are married. One of the problems occurs because Medicaid considers all assets of a husband and wife to be owned equally. That means that you can't protect your assets by having them in the name of the stay-at-home spouse. So transferring them into the other spouse's name won't help. That is where we begin.

Under current law, while there is no limit on the amount of assets that can be transferred from one spouse to the other, there is a limit in the amount the stay-at-home spouse may retain and still qualify the other spouse for Medicaid. These figures depend upon your state of residence and are adjusted annually for inflation.

We talked about the house previously. In the case of a married couple, Medicaid currently *does* allow the stay-at-home spouse to keep the home. And unlike other assets, Medicaid does allow it to be transferred into the name of the stay-at-home spouse. Although the stay-at-home spouse may not transfer it as long as the other spouse is in the nursing home, the house may be conveyed at the death of the stay-at-home spouse.

On the other hand, if the stay-at-home spouse dies while his or her spouse is still in the nursing home, then the home will most likely pass to the confined spouse. When that spouse dies, then Medicaid will try to collect what it has paid.

Protecting your assets

Many people get upset at the prospect of losing everything they've worked for to a nursing home stay. Instead, they try to qualify themselves for Medicaid by divesting themselves of assets. The two ways people have chosen to do this is in the past was either by giving them away or putting them in an irrevocable trust. Before we look at each, let's look at the general rule Medicaid follows concerning the transfer of assets.

The 1993 tax act, officially known as the Omnibus Budget Reconciliation Act of 1993 (OBRA), put a huge dent in the planning of middle-class citizens attempting to protect their assets from a prolonged nursing home stay. Any transfers made prior to the August 11, 1993, should fall under the old law. Any transfers after that date, however, will be subject to the following rules.

Caution: Because this is a new law, it is subject to modification. Be sure you work with a knowledgable attorney before taking any action.

Look-back period. The government realizes that many people will give their assets away to avoid losing them to a nursing home stay. Obviously, they can't allow people to do this and still automatically qualify for Medicaid. Therefore, a "look-back" period applies. This is the time that must elapse between the time you give your assets away and the time you apply for Medicaid. The 1993 tax act increased that period from 30 to 36 months for transfers to individuals, and 60 months for transfers into an irrevocable trust.

Ineligibility period. Under the old law, if you applied for Medicaid before the 30-month time period elapsed, then all you had to do was wait until the balance of the 30 months passed before Medicaid kicked in. The new law is totally different. If you apply for Medicaid prior to the end of the 36-month period, you must pay for your nursing home care for a period that will effectively exhaust the transferred assets.

The law states that this period is calculated by dividing the value of the transferred assets by your state's average monthly cost of a nursing home. For example, if you transfer $150,000 and your state's rate is $2,000, you will have to pay another 75 months ($150,000 divided by $2,000) beyond the date you apply for Medicaid.

You can see that applying for Medicaid too soon can be an expensive mistake. This problem can be avoided by following this rule: *If the value of the assets you transferred exceeds 36 times your state's official rate, don't apply for Medicaid until the 36-month period has passed.*

Giving your assets away

One way to remove assets from your estate is by giving them away, presumably to your children. This can be done by writing a check, transferring the title on your property from your name to theirs, etc. However, this brings up several problems.

- If the transfer is for less than fair market value and is made within 36 months of your entering a nursing home, you will run up against the rules noted above.
- Once you give those assets away, you have no right to them whatsoever. You are not entitled to any part of them. Those assets belong to your children to do with as they see fit.
- You may run into the gift tax problems discussed earlier in the book. However, if your estate is under $600,000 and you haven't used any of your exemption previously, this will not cause a problem. But you must file a gift tax return.

There is an exception to the ineligibility period. If you transfer property to a spouse, disabled child or caretaker child, the transfer is exempt.

Putting them into a Medicaid Trust

In the past, many individuals chose to put their assets into a Medicaid Trust. Using this tool, the individual could remove assets from his or her estate, but still receive income from the trust. The effectiveness of the trust has been restricted by the new tax law for two reasons. First, the look-back period for assets transferred into an irrevocable trust has been extended to 60 months. Second, in all but a few cases, the new law treats assets in a trust from which you receive any benefits as available for paying nursing home expenses. This removes your ability to "have your cake and eat it, too."

Recovery

The 1993 tax act requires that all states attempt to recover the expenses paid by Medicaid. This is a major change, in that previous law left this up to each individual state. This part of the law applies to Medicaid expenses paid after October 1, 1993.

Each state must determine how they are going to recover the money. In addition, there will be further determination on exactly what can be recovered. However it appears that most assets are at risk.

Conclusion

As you can see, a nursing home stay poses problems with few good solutions. However, as bad as the alternatives may sound, they are still better than doing nothing. You risk your entire asset base by refusing to plan. If you wait too long, it may be too late.

This is such an important and specialized area that it *requires* proper planning with the proper advisor. Don't try to do it yourself. Don't rely on friends for advice. Unfortunately, there are only a few attorneys who understand the problems and the solutions. But find one. You need professional assistance. Please, don't wait and hope.

Twenty-Six

What About Living Wills and Health Care Powers?

Our definition of estate planning starts out with the words, "During my life..." This chapter deals with several planning methods that take care of you during your life: the living will and health care powers.

Living will

The living will often gets confused with the living trust, but they have no similarities. The *living will* is the document in which you indicate your desire *not* to be kept alive by life support equipment. I don't need to tell you that medical technology has increased life expectancy. Living longer, however, doesn't necessarily mean the quality of life has improved. There are many cases when people are kept alive solely by life support equipment.

The Supreme Court has ruled that if you want "live or not live" decisions made for you, you must have that permission clearly indicated. The living will allows you to do that. Unfortunately, only 20 percent of the population has one.

The purpose of the living will (also known as an advanced directive or advanced medical directive) is to allow you to let your desires be known concerning life support equipment. In other words, a living will indicates that you do not wish to be kept alive only by a machine. It effectively says "If I am only being kept alive by a machine, unplug it."

Understand that the laws vary state to state. In fact, many states have their own living will form that must be followed. Check with your attorney and make sure that your living will conforms to your state guidelines. If you spend time in other states, you might also want to check on their requirements. This is an extremely important issue and well worth your time and effort.

Health care powers

While the living will makes a lot of sense, it does have its drawbacks. It does not address the issue of medical decisions that may or may not prolong one's life.

Grace McIntyre was in the hospital with a stroke. She wasn't given much of a chance to live, but the doctors felt they had to do all they could for her. Although there was virtually no chance for improvement, the doctors tried operation after operation. She had a living will, but that didn't help—she was not being kept alive by life support equipment. She was just being put through many operations that had little chance for success, operations that depleted her assets. All her suffering, and that of her family, was for naught. She ran out of money about the same time that she passed away.

This is an example of a situation where a living will had no benefit. The decision was not one of unplugging a machine. The decision was about performing operations that had little hope of helping her.

As a result, about 80 percent of the states have adopted some form of a new document: The Durable Power of Attorney for Health Care (called Health Care Proxies in certain states).

With this document, you actually appoint someone to make medical decisions for you. That person has the authority to turn down a surgical procedure that is of questionable value. While it is your physician's duty to keep you alive, many procedures don't have much of a success rate. The Durable Power for Health Care addresses that issue.

As with the appointment of the trustees of a trust, you will want to appoint successor agents. You never know when one person can't, or won't, be able to make the necessary decisions.

In some cases, you can leave specific instructions about what you do and do not want done to or for you. You can discuss such issues as feeding, transfusions, transplants, etc. If your state allows it, leave as many instructions as you can.

In some states, the health care power replaces the living will, since it is a more comprehensive form. In other states, you need both forms. As with the living will, many states have their own forms and sets of rules concerning the durable power for health care. You cannot assume that what is acceptable in Missouri is acceptable in Maine. In some cases, the legislature has specified the exact language that must be used. As with the living will, check with your attorney for the rules in your state.

Caution

One problem with these documents is that they don't do much good if you don't have them with you when you go into a hospital. The doctor, without any other instructions, is obligated to do whatever he or she can to keep you alive. And once started, it's difficult to reverse the process. There are several ways you might solve this problem.

- Have "duplicate originals" of the form filed with your physicians, local hospitals, agents (those who can make decisions for you) and attorney. Make sure your patient records reflect your wishes.
- Carry a form when you travel. While it might not be honored in another state, it will at least contain your wishes.
- Carry a letter or note in your wallet indicating that you have a form and where it can be found.

Another important point is to make sure that the persons you appoint as your agents will follow your wishes. There are many people who would never, under any circumstances, make the decision to end another's life, even if it is what that person wanted. Having the wrong person in the decision-making position will totally invalidate the benefit of the form.

Finally, check with your attorney about the expiration date of the form. Some states have specific requirements dealing with this aspect. It may be valid forever—it may be valid only three years.

This is a very difficult issue to address. Many people ignore it and hope it will go away. But you know better than that. Modern medicine, with all its fantastic advances, can be a burden on you and your family. Take the initiative and make your wishes known. You may only have one opportunity to do it—do it now!

Twenty-Seven

How Can I Protect My Assets From a Lawsuit?

by Kelly R. Burke, Attorney-at-Law

How often have you heard about a businessman who has filed bankruptcy but does not seem to lose anything in the process? Bankruptcy was formerly a devastating, last-gasp step. Now bankruptcy is so commonplace, some people walk into bankruptcy court with their prepared "plan" in place.

Most doctors, lawyers, architects, engineers, business owners, real estate developers and other professionals (called the *"provider"* for this discussion), for moral or professional reasons would not consider bankruptcy except in the most drastic of situations. Nevertheless, most of them would like to limit their asset exposure.

Business owners and professionals are not the only ones at risk today. One of the more unfortunate aspects of society today is what appears to be a glut of lawsuits, many of which appear to be baseless. And it is not just the doctor or businessperson who has to be concerned. It is the baseball coach who gets sued by a parent, or the boy scout leader who has an unhappy camper, or the dog owner whose lovable pet attacks the neighbor's daughter. When we discuss lawsuit protection, we are not just talking about product liability claims or malpractice suits, we are talking about substantial claims against everyday citizens.

Proper estate planning contemplates that you have an estate for which to plan. If you fail to protect that estate, then all your planning goes for naught. So let us take a look at lawsuit protection and see what steps you might consider.

Assets lost

I have always felt that the best explanation of legal principles is to avoid citing case law, statutes and IRS regulations. Instead I think the best explanation of asset protection is by example (or "war stories" as attorneys call them). Because state law varies tremendously, realize that this discussion is only general in nature.

Paul Marcus, a successful securities defense lawyer, had built up a large portfolio of assets and had a net worth of $5 million. While Paul was one of the best in his field, like most attorneys, he had no experience or education in estate planning. Paul and his wife, Ann, were looking forward to Paul's retirement so that they could tour the world. Over the years, Paul had titled all of his assets in his name. Shortly before his retirement, Paul made an error on a new issue of stock, thus resulting in liabilities and SEC fines of millions of dollars against him and his firm. Paul had professional liability insurance, but due to the trebling nature of the SEC fines, his personal assets were subject to the judgment that followed and rendered him virtually penniless.

*   *   *

McNab's Roofing, a successful home improvement company, was owned solely by Larry McNab. One day, workers were putting a new roof on an older home when a package of shingles slid off the roof, landing on the homeowner's 13-year old son. The resulting injury led to a multimillion dollar lawsuit against Mr. McNab. The jury agreed with the plaintiffs and found against McNab Roofing. The company did not have sufficient liability insurance to cover the judgment. As a result, since he was a sole proprietorship, Larry McNab was responsible for the balance of the judgment. This wiped him out personally and resulted in his filing personal bankruptcy. All his life's work was gone.

*   *   *

Norman Randall, John Pierce and Brian Walters were each one-third partners in a real estate development company. Although most of the deals were developed by all three partners, on occasion one or two of the partners would do a deal separately. Such was the case when John borrowed substantial dollars to build a mall. Unfortunately, the financing fell through when the savings and loan failed. John was on the hook for substantial dollars to the contractors, suppliers, utilities, etc. Try as he might, John could not get additional financing. Work stopped and suits were filed. The fact that

212

John lost everything is not surprising. What shocked Norm and Brian was that the court found that John had represented that the partnership was involved. And they further found that Norm and Brian did not take any action to indicate that they were not involved. As a result, the three were found individually liable for John's debts. John lost everything. Norm and Brian were a little more fortunate— they retained approximately 15 percent of their net worth. Obviously, the partnership is no more.

*   *   *

Bill Richmond, a local businessman and past-president of the chamber of commerce was married to a woman 20 years his junior. Bill was worth approximately $3 million on top of his business which was worth another million. Being a do-it-yourselfer, Bill decided he would "protect" his assets from liability by placing all of them in his wife's name. He retitled all his personal assets into Carol's name and set up a closely held corporation (owned by Carol) to hold his business equipment, inventory and land. The corporation, in turn, leased everything back to Bill's business. The fact that Bill had no control over where his assets would go upon his death is one matter. The real problem now is that Bill had no control over his assets while he was alive.

Bill, in his capacity as president of the chamber of commerce, took a month-long trip to Europe to scout for business. Carol could not go, having "prior commitments." Bill returned home and looked for his lovely wife at the airport. Not finding her, Bill called home only to be told the phone had been disconnected. The chauffeur took Bill to his house. The current residents expressed shock that Bill thought he owned this house. After all, they had just closed on it last week. Where was the lovely Carol? She and the club tennis pro were having the time of their lives in Rio.

At least Bill had his business, right? Well, Carol needed the assistance of a lawyer to help her dispose of her assets quickly. It seems that the lease payments were his fee. Cannot happen? Think again.

When I relate these cases, some say that they sound a little far-fetched. What these people do not realize is that these are some of the more common cases. You would be shocked as to some more bizarre cases I have seen.

Historically, *providers* tend not to worry too much about liability because: 1) they do not think they are at risk; 2) they have liability insurance; and 3) they want to retain control over their assets.

Typically, those who do attempt asset protection usually do so by titling their assets in the name of their spouse. But as reflected in Bill Richmond's case, that can be hazardous.

What actions can you take to protect assets? For the purposes of this discussion, I have narrowed it down to the three most effective and common methods: incorporation, living trusts and family limited partnerships.

Incorporation

Our economy operates as a "free-market" capitalistic marketplace. It is based on businesses that provide a service or product, hopefully for a profit. Owning a business is not, of course, without risk. In addition to the risk of losing your investment, you can be sued and lose everything you have.

Before beginning our discussion of asset protection, let's briefly compare the three primary forms of businesses used today: sole proprietorships, partnerships, and corporations.

Sole Proprietorship is the most common form of ownership. It occurs when a business is owned by one person, as are most small businesses in this country. It has the advantage of being simple to organize, with a minimum of legal regulations and paperwork. Taxes are filed as part of the income tax return on a Schedule C. However, the big disadvantage as shown by Larry McNab's case, is that the sole proprietor is personally liable for any debts or actions of the business.

Partnerships are essentially the same as sole proprietorships, with the main difference being that there are two or more owners. There is a little more paperwork in that partnership agreements must be established. Additionally, profits and losses are allocated directly to the partners in relation to their ownership. However, like the sole proprietorship, there is no liability protection for the individual owners. The case involving the real estate development firm reflected the big hazard: The individual partners were liable for the action of the other partners, and not just in proportion to their ownership. There is one form of partnership, the family limited partnership, which we will be discussing shortly, which does provide liability protection.

Corporations represent the smallest number of businesses in the country, but those businesses account for the largest segment of sales. The corporation is a legal entity with stockholders, articles of incorporation, bylaws, annual meetings, etc. Papers are filed within that state to become "incorporated." From that point, it operates as a separate entity. Corporations offer an advantage in that the shareholders have limited liability, though directors and officers are facing greater exposure today. In most states, laws are being passed allowing directors protection from the majority of lawsuits out there.

Types of Corporations

For tax considerations, there two types of corporations: "S" and "C." The "C" corporation is the normal structure for major companies. They file a separate tax return and pay their taxes at the corporate rate. Based on the 1993 tax law, the corporate rate is advantageous if earnings are below $50,000. Above that, rates are relatively equal. One of the big disadvantages for a "C" corporation is that income can be double-taxed. The corporation pays tax when it earns it. Then again when distributed via dividends to shareholders. This entire structure can be a burden for small businesses.

To provide the advantages of corporations without the double taxation, Congress in 1958 came up with a new type of corporation, the "Subchapter S," now referred to as "S." These are for small businesses who meet the following qualifications (subject to change):

* No more than 35 shareholders
* Stockholders are individuals, estates or specific trusts
* Only one class of stock

From a liability standpoint, the rules are the same: The individual stockholders are not personally liable for the debts of the corporation. We can see how things might have been different had Larry McNab been incorporated.

Larry McNab, the roofing company owner, lost everything because, as a sole proprietorship, he was personally liable for the acts of his employees. Had his company been incorporated, he would not have personally lost anything. Of course, the corporation itself could have lost all its assets, but that certainly would be a better alternative than the loss of all of his personal assets.

One word of warning. There are many rules and regulations that relate to corporations. They cannot be operated as a personal pocket-book. The corporation must file the proper papers, hold the proper meetings, and not co-mingle the funds with personal use. If those procedures are not followed precisely, then the corporate shield can be pierced and personal assets placed at risk.

Living trusts

Steve has devoted substantial space to living trusts in this book. I agree with him that living trusts are the preferred form of planning in most estate planning cases. As an attorney, I see what happens in probate court. I see the problems families face that literally tear them apart. And I see the wasted dollars going to my brothers and sisters in the legal profession.

Much of the earlier discussion of living trusts revolved around the advantages, disadvantages, structure, etc. What I want to cover is the use of living trusts as an asset-protection method.

While as a rule it is true that revocable living trusts do not provide asset protection, there is one area that I have found very effective with my clients. What Bill Richmond tried to do was the right idea. Unfortunately, the way he decided to do it meant that he lost control. In my experience, control is a very important factor to business owners. Wouldn't it be great if you could place your assets in your spouse's name, maintain control and still be protected against lawsuits? You can—with a properly drawn trust.

Remember some basic tenets of living trusts: Assets are placed in a trust by a trustmaker; trustees are appointed to manage these assets; beneficiaries reap the benefits of the trust. Under normal circumstances, all three positions are occupied by the same person, usually the husband and wife. However, with that structure, *none* of the assets are protected from creditors of either trustmaker.

Thus, the only way to possibly protect those assets is *not* to occupy all three positions (again, due to varying state laws, advice of legal counsel is always required). This means that you cannot set up a trust the "normal" way, which is with a joint trust with each spouse as co-trustee with some degree of control over the property. In this situation, there is no asset protection.

Instead, let us establish separate trusts for each spouse. Here is how it works:

- Separate trusts are established; one for the spouse with liability concerns (called the *"provider"*) and one for the other spouse (called the *"spouse"*).
- Both the *spouse and provider* are co-trustees of the *spouse's* trust.
- Only the *provider* is trustee of the *provider's* trust.
- The *provider* conveys his or her property to the *spouse*, who then places the property into his or her separate trust. Thus, the trust property is the "property" of the *spouse*, and is not subject to the creditors of the *provider*. It is just as though the *spouse* had full ownership.

The difference, and the advantage, of the revocable living trust over regular ownership is that the *provider* still maintains control over the property by virtue of being co-trustee of the *spouse's* trust. Remember that the trustees control and manage the property in the trust estate for the beneficiaries. But the trustees have no right to the trust assets, only the right to exercise management over the trust assets.

The beneficiaries are the only persons entitled to use, spend and enjoy the trust assets since the trustees have no right to the benefit of the trust property. This brings up the other major complaint from most providers, "I do not want to give up my assets, I worked hard for this." That is why an irrevocable trust is generally out of the question, except in certain limited situations. Yet the *provider can be the beneficiary of the spouse's <u>revocable</u> living trust!* A revocable living trust can name both spouses, children, parents, etc., as the beneficiaries. The *provider* gets to enjoy the fruit of his or her labor, yet because ownership is in the *spouse's* trust, the *provider* need not worry about losing his or her assets to the birds of prey patrolling the local courtrooms.

Recall the examples set out earlier? How would those situations have been affected by a properly drawn, revocable living trust? Let's look:

Paul, the securities lawyer, lost his fortune because he owned his assets in his name. If Paul had given the assets to his wife, and a living trust was created in Ann's name with both of them as joint trustees, Paul would have protected "his" assets from the SEC fines and malpractice claim because he would have had no ownership interest in the assets. Yet he would have had control over the assets as joint trustee with his wife. Paul would have been able to take that trip around the world upon his retirement.

This same technique could be helpful for any professional concerned with a malpractice suit. By titling the assets in the spouse's name, they would not be part of the professional's assets. Yet, if the professional is co-trustee of that trust, then he or she can still maintain some control.

*　　　*　　　*

Bill was the businessman with the young wife. He could have placed his personal assets in his wife's name, with the assets immediately going into a living trust with Bill and Carol as joint trustees. All the assets would have been creditor-free, at least from Bill's liability claims (Carol's creditors would have been another thing, but the risk/benefit has to be in Carol's favor). Since Bill would have been a joint trustee with Carol, she would not have been able to sell the house from underneath John when he went to Europe. Carol might have left with the club tennis pro, but at least not with Bill's money in tow.

By the way, not all joint trustees have to co-sign each check. The rules can be adjusted for different circumstances, just like corporate checks. One can set up a procedure where checks for less than $500 (or whatever figure you want) can go through without two signatures. Bankers can provide the type of check-writing privileges needed for a trust.

Larry McNab, the roofing company owner, besides forming a corporation, could have had all his personal assets owned by his wife's living trust. Although the corporation would have lost all its assets, he would have retained his.

Normally, not all of the assets belonging to the *provider* will be placed in the *spouse's* name. Depending on state law, some assets have to be "owned" by the professional (i.e., professional corporation stock). Another consideration is the use of the $600,000 federal estate tax exemption. The *provider* needs to pass his or her $600,000 to someone other than the surviving spouse (this is where the family trust comes into play) to maximize estate tax planning. That might be done by passing assets with minimal value to litigious parties to the family trust. For example: the closely held stock, life insurance proceeds, retirement plan assets, etc. By limiting the amount subject to creditors to $600,000, and making those assets the hardest type of assets against which to collect, the *provider* has deterred the collection of the judgment and might encourage a settlement with the creditor.

However, a living trust is not perfect. First, the trustmaking spouse can "fire" the co-trustee, thus creating the possibility that the *spouse* can fire the *provider* and do whatever he or she wants to do anyway. The properly drawn trust will have some type of notice provision (typically 30 days) that requires notice to the "fired" trustee (*provider*). This will at least give the *provider* time to take appropriate action to thwart the coming storm.

Further, since the trust is revocable, which is more often beneficial than detrimental, it can technically be canceled by the *spouse* while the *provider* is on a trip. In practice this is very complex and unrealistic. Virtually every stock brokerage firm, bank and real estate lawyer would require notice to the nonconsenting trustee. A joint trustee clause on a stock brokerage account is an "and" account, requiring both signatures. Did you ever try to close or clean out an "and" account without both signatures? If you got lucky and did so, the entity that allowed it might be liable if you were without proper authorization. Most institutions, likewise, would subscribe to the rule that when revoking a trust, both trustees have to consent to transfers or major dispositions of assets. Therefore it is, as a practical matter, inconceivable that the spouse could revoke the trust and disburse assets without proper authorization from the other trustee. At a minimum, he or she would have to be in compliance with the notice provisions stated earlier.

Finally, depending again on state law, and to some extent federal law, the transfers to the revocable living trusts contemplated earlier would generally need to be created two years or more before the liability (or as lawyers, say "cause of action") arose. Thus, you cannot create a trust after you know of the liability. In order to take advantage of the trust benefits as to liability, you need to create the trust now before these future problems arise. This is very similar to insurance: you cannot buy life insurance once you have been diagnosed as having a terminal condition. Most people wait until the problem occurs before doing anything, but in each example set out earlier, the providers did not realize they had problems until it was too late. That is why this is called estate *planning*!

Weighing the good against the bad, the advantages of a revocable living trust far outweigh the drawbacks. No matter what, it certainly beats the alternatives. You will complicate the search for personal assets by litigious claimants, protect against the disappearing spouse (at least disappearing with your money!), and you will, I suspect, be able to sleep a little better at night. There is no substitute for peace of mind. Trusts do not solve every problem, but they do solve most.

Family limited partnerships

The use of family limited partnerships (FLPs) as an income tax and estate tax reduction method was discussed in Chapter 21. However, there is another use of these unique vehicles: to provide tremendous liability protection to you and your family.

As discussed earlier, partnerships are a form of ownership between two or more persons. They have two classes of owners. The distinction is as follows:

General partners run the partnership. They make all the decisions, receive a salary for their efforts, and are liable for the debts of the partnership. Additionally, they can (if authorized by the partnership agreement), decide not to make any distributions to the limited partners. This is what will make it so powerful as liability protection.

Limited partners are the "silent" partners. They have no say in the day-to-day operations, receive no salary, but they are entitled to a share of the partnership distributions as declared by the general partner. And, most important, they are protected against creditors to the extent of their original investment.

Earlier in this chapter, we discussed the advantages of incorporation and living trusts. But there are still assets at risk. Using an FLP will add one more layer of protection. The easiest way to illustrate this is to look at some earlier examples.

Larry and his wife could have established the McNab Family Partnership. This entity could have consisted of a 1-percent general partner interest and a 99-percent limited partnership interest. Larry could have been the general partner and his wife's living trust could have been the limited partner. If they had wanted even more protection, they could have formed a new corporation to be the general partner, however this corporation should be a legitimate business operation. When the corporation got sued, his personal assets would have been protected. And if either he or his wife were somehow found liable for the acts of the corporation, this second corporation and FLP could have given even more protection.

The question that invariably comes up is: "What is to keep the creditor from going after the money in the limited partnership?" Here is the really interesting part. In most cases, when a judgment is issued against a family limited partnership, all the creditor receives is a "charging order." This effectively makes him or her a lienholder on the partnership, not an actual limited partner. They would have no rights to attach any of the assets of the partnership.

But that is only part of the story. In addition to not being able to touch any of the assets, current IRS regulations require them to pay taxes on any income generated by the partnership, *although they would not actually be receiving any income.* This would certainly deter their action against the partnership!

Understand, however, that FLPs have a strict set of rules that must be followed, and that attempts to defraud creditors will be seen as such. Nevertheless, they can confuse the issue and throw up so many roadblocks that they can be effective devices to protect assets.

Let's revisit Bill Richmond, the businessman with the young wife. We talked earlier about placing his assets into his wife's trust. Of course, that still would have resulted in some problems. What if, instead, his assets were in his FLP, with himself as 1-percent general partner and his wife 99-percent limited partner? Obviously, if Carol decided to leave, he would have had a few problems. But, beyond that, he could have really made things difficult for his wife. Since she owned the limited partnership interest, she could have taken it with her. However, Bill could have pulled a fast one on her. As general partner, he could have decided that no distributions were to be made. However, he could still receive a salary as the general partner. But what would make it unbearable on his wife would be that, as limited partner, she would be responsible for declaring her 99 percent of the partnership income as her personal income, although she would not be receiving it. The power of FLPs is astounding!

Of course, FLPs are not without their disadvantages. They are expensive to establish and do not guarantee absolute protection to your assets. Nevertheless, they will give you a greater degree of safety than anything else we have discussed.

Conclusion

One final word of caution. Ever wonder why they call it the "practice" of law? There are some lawyers who do "practice" on their clients. Despite insufficient training, experience and requisite legal knowledge, many lawyers will draw up a will or even a trust. So be sure to get competent legal advice. Do not let the lawyer practice on *you*; you have worked too hard to get where you are.

Another major complaint from the public is that lawyers draw up documents that only lawyers understand. (Yet, if that were true, why do so many people end up in court arguing over what a signed contract really means? Even lawyers sometimes do not know what their own verbiage means, which is why they make such good senators.) If required to do so, lawyers can make a document easily readable. So make sure you understand what the planning document says and means, every single word of it.

Part V

Special Planning
Situations

Twenty-Eight

What Happens to My Business Upon My Death?

One of the more difficult issues I encounter when working with business owners/doctors/farmers is the question of what will happen to their businesses/professional practices/farms upon their deaths. They want to ensure that their heirs receive full value and that estate taxes won't eat up the asset. This is an area that is very complex because it brings together so many factors and involves a myriad of planning issues. Unfortunately, like so many issues we have discussed, the complexity and amount of thought required means that most people don't plan at all.

Why is planning so important?

Small businesses represent a vital cog in our economic cycle, although you'd have a tough time telling it from the way Congress treats the small businessperson. Family businesses generate 40 percent of the gross national product. They represent 95 percent of all businesses in this country. They employ a significant portion of the work force. Yet, because of improper planning, fewer than 33 percent survive the second generation, and of those, only 50 percent make it to the third generation. Considering the amount of work that went into the business by the founder, that is a sad commentary. Even sadder, however, is the fact that this is completely unnecessary. Proper planning could dramatically increase those statistics.

What will happen at your death?

Many people have devoted the bulk of their lives to building a business/professional practice/farm. They have spent untold thousands of dollars making that endeavor a success. Yet, very little time is expended on considering what will happen to that effort upon the death of one of the principals.

Michael Law was a general surgeon who had been in solo practice for many years. He always felt the value of his practice was based on his ability as a surgeon. He realized that he had no equipment of consequence for his wife to sell. His practice didn't provide a flow of repeat patients. As a result, his planning was based upon having sufficient life insurance to take care of his wife, while assuming the value of his practice would be virtually nothing. However, there was one thing he didn't plan on: his wife dying first. Then, upon his subsequent death, his heirs received their inheritance. They also received a shock when they learned that the value of his medical practice was included in his estate. This resulted in unexpected estate taxes. Though the practice had no ongoing value to the heirs, the IRS didn't agree that it was worthless. In fact, the IRS attached such a high value that the bulk of Dr. Law's estate was eaten up by estate taxes.

*   *   *

C.B. Franklin owned a farm that had been in his family since the early 1900s. It had survived the Depression and all the activity that occurred around it as a major metropolitan area continued to spread. The farm had been passed down from generation to generation. When C.B.'s brother died several years ago, C.B. inherited his half. While he never thought about any estate taxes that might be due at his brother's death, the real problem occurred when the IRS ruled that his farm did not qualify as an active farm because less than half the land was used for farming. Therefore, it was valued at its actual market value, which was high because it could be developed for residential use.

*   *   *

Roger Adamson was a 25-percent stockholder in Midwest Manufacturing Company. It was a closely held corporation in which his other partners owned 40 percent, 20 percent and 15 percent respectively. While they had thought about succession planning, it never was of much concern. The corporation was profitable. All the partners realized that they could continue the business upon the death of

225

any of the others. So, when Roger died, his wife inherited his stock. She had no interest in participating in the business, and his former partners certainly didn't want her involved. However, she soon found out that the company had made no plans for this eventuality. They all soon realized that the worst was yet to come.

*   *   *

Hank Warren, a widower, was sole owner of a successful service company. He had three children, Jonathan, Ben and Wendy. Jonathan worked with him in the family business; Ben and Wendy were each married and living in other cities. Hank had always assumed that Jonathan would take over the business. He had a good head on his shoulders and a feel for what it took to be successful. The company had borrowed substantial amounts of money. Hank was on all the notes; Jonathan on some. When Hank died, his will was read. He left everything to his children, one-third each. All of a sudden, Jonathan was a minority stockholder in the business his father wanted him to have.

These are just a few cases illustrating the problems that individuals face upon their deaths. As the statistics stated previously show, these cases are not unique.

Valuation

If your heirs are going to receive full value for your business/practice/farm, you first need to determine the value. This is an inexact science if there ever was one. What you think it is worth can be vastly different from what the IRS thinks. What you can sell it for today may not be an indication of its true value. Its current use may not represent what the IRS decides. The operative organization here is the Internal Revenue Service. It pronounces the final verdict—the only one that matters.

Since we are talking about businesses, medical and dental practices, and farms, let's explore each and look at the valuation problems and issues.

Closely held business. A closely held business differs from a public company, such as Wal-Mart, in that there is no readily established market value for the stock. Whereas Wal-Mart is traded on the

New York Stock Exchange and is easy to value at any given time, the same isn't true with Midwest Manufacturing Company (our first example of this chapter). Because there is no ready market for the stock, meaning no exchange where the stock is bought and sold, valuation is difficult.

But before talking about the problems, let's first see why there is a question of valuation in the first place. Why is it so important?

Beyond the obvious answer that valuation is important for financial planning reasons, there are two factors that are important from the standpoint of this book.

- Upon your death, or the death of any of the stockholders, the deceased's interest is usually sold. Proper valuation helps determine that price and makes any transition less of a burden.
- Upon the death of a shareholder, the value of his or her stock is included in the estate for federal estate tax purposes. It is important to know what this valuation is for estate tax liquidity purposes.

Because several valuation methods are used, precise figures are difficult. For example, the value might be based on book value, capitalization of average earnings, book value plus goodwill, or fair market value plus a multiple of past earnings. Since there are so many different methods, many planners and CPAs average the various methods together to reach a final figure.

Further, it is important to take advantage of any special valuations that are permitted under our tax code. For example, special gift tax valuation rules are permitted in situations in which business interests are transferred to members of one's family. It is important to seek knowledgeable counsel in this area.

Farm. The case earlier in this chapter reflects several good reasons why it is so important to properly value farms in advance. In situations where I have worked with farmers, they have tended to downplay the value of their farm. They usually complain about the problems they have making money and assume that factor will have a major bearing on the valuation of their farm. And while it is a consideration, it is not necessarily the overriding one.

On the other hand, there are some breaks for farmers or ranchers that will help them from an estate tax standpoint. Included in this is a "special use valuation," which allows the valuation on its "current" use rather than on the basis of "highest and best" use. However, there are restrictions and limitations that must be taken into consideration. Unfortunately, this didn't help in our example.

Medical/Dental Practice. The medical and dental professions are unique. While most businesses have a tangible product that gives value to the business, the professional only has himself or herself. As a result, valuing a practice can be difficult. Unlike a business, which has value beyond one or two individuals, a medical or dental practice is based almost solely on the reputation and competence of the individual practitioner. Again, it is important to work with advisors who specialize in this area to help you with your valuation.

Potential problems

In dealing in this area, there are some problems that constantly crop up. They are not unique. They need not be a surprise. They are just the result of lack of planning.

Like so much we have discussed thus far, problems can be resolved when they are anticipated. But business people, farmers and doctors are so busy running their businesses or professions that they rarely take the time to do meaningful planning. Hopefully, this will change.

Unforeseen estate taxes. Dr. Law's children were faced with a surprise. The sole practitioner rarely considers estate taxes because he or she doesn't regard the practice as having sufficient value to cause concern. As a result, he or she usually goes ahead with financial plans and lets the chips fall where they may.

Nevertheless, estate taxes can be an issue. Normally, this is not a problem if the practitioner is survived by a spouse, because no estate taxes are due at the first death. By the time the surviving spouse is gone, the practice is long forgotten and not a tax issue.

But if the practitioner has no spouse, or if both spouses die simultaneously, there is a problem that must be addressed. That practice, at least as far as the IRS is concerned, has value, although in reality that practice is limited once the sole practitioner has died. But try to tell that to the IRS. They will value it as they see fit.

Dr. Michael Law survived his wife. The value of his estate, not including his practice, was $2 million. At his death, the IRS valued his practice at $750,000. As a result, this valuation increased his federal estate taxes from approximately $588,000 to $965,500. Though his practice had no value to his children, they had to pay significant taxes. Proper planning could have avoided this problem.

*   *   *

For C.B. Franklin, taxes were a complete surprise. While he had considered that there might be some taxes due, he certainly couldn't predict the disastrous results. C.B. Franklin's farm is located in a fast-growing section of a major metropolitan area. There are subdivisions and office parks surrounding his 100-plus acres. And, due to his age, he is farming very little of the land. The IRS says the land should be taxed at its actual market value. That means that Mr. Franklin's brother's estate will have to pay over $500,000 in estate taxes—liquid cash that is just not available.

Lack of funds. The case of Roger Adamson is not unique. Many business people and medical practitioners with whom I counsel never make any plans for the death of one of the stockholders. That was the case at Midwest Manufacturing.

The stockholders were too busy making money to think about potential problems. Everything seemed to be going so well. And since they were all relatively young, they never anticipated a death. So when Roger died, his wife inherited his stock. She was now a minority stockholder in a closely held corporation. And she was willing to sell her stock back to Midwest...for a price. She certainly wasn't greedy, she just wanted fair value. She retained an attorney, and a settlement was negotiated. Midwest, being a fast-growing company, didn't have the cash with which to pay her. So her attorney drafted an agreement under which she would be paid monthly for a period of five years. She signed over her stock to the corporation in exchange for a promissory note, collateralized by that very stock and certain equipment and inventory.

All of a sudden, the corporation had a debt on its balance sheet. It also had a cash flow drain—she was getting money and contributing nothing for it. They also had to hire someone to take Roger's place. This changed the entire picture within the corporation. The situation caused a strain on everyone that could have been easily avoided at a minimal expense.

No provisions for the family business. For Jonathan Warren and his sister and brother, things couldn't have been worse. They all became equal owners of a business that only Jonathan understood and cared about. Ben and Wendy had established their own careers. They just weren't interested in the family business. But they did feel they were entitled to their portion of their father's estate. Since together they were majority stockholders, Ben and Wendy wanted a voice in the business—and some income from it. It turned into a total disaster. The bankers were scared enough when Hank died. Now they panicked. The kids never got along too well anyway. Now they were continually feuding. The bankers saw what was happening to the business and, one by one, they called the loans. The company had to sell equipment to pay back the banks. Finally, the business filed bankruptcy. It is a business no more.

Loan guarantees result in gift and estate taxes. As discussed previously, if you guarantee a loan for another, that act is now interpreted by the IRS as a gift to that person. Any guarantee over $10,000 (your annual gift exclusion) will require that you file a gift tax return and reduce your $600,000 lifetime exemption for guarantees over your annual exclusion. This is true even if the guarantee is never exercised.

In addition, those guarantees can have adverse estate tax consequences if you wish to leave property to a spouse under the unlimited marital deduction. For a complete discussion of this problem, refer to Chapter 15.

Solutions

All these cases have one thing in common: lack of planning. In the Law case, the family ended up paying needless taxes. In the Franklin case, this nice gentleman is faced with losing his farm. In the Adamson case, the business ended up paying out money needlessly. In the Warren case, no provisions were made for passing the business. The sad fact is that each and every one of these devastating situations could have been avoided with some simple planning.

The bulk of this book has been spent discussing smooth transitions, usually from family member to family member, and eliminating unhappy surprises. Remember our definition:

"During my life and after my death, I want to control and distribute my property in the manner I desire, minimizing all fees, taxes and court interference, preserving for myself, my family, and those I choose, the estate I have worked so hard to create."

Did any of our examples accomplish this? No. Because, once again, all the people planned for the best by not planning at all. What are the possible solutions? Let's look.

Buy-sell agreements

One of the easiest ways to solve many business succession problems is with a buy-sell agreement. That was certainly true in the case of Midwest Manufacturing.

A buy-sell agreement is a written agreement whereby one party agrees to sell and another party or parties agree to buy it. The sale takes place at a predetermined price (or based on a predetermined formula) and takes effect upon death of one of the stockholders. It is the ideal vehicle to guarantee continuity.

There are three types of buy-sell agreements.

1. Cross-purchase. This agreement is entered into between the various shareholders. Each partner agrees with the other to purchase his or her share for (typically) a predetermined price. This agreement is binding on all the parties, including the heirs. In our case, Roger's share would have been purchased in proportion by each of his surviving partners.

This type of agreement has the advantage of creating a market, which previously didn't exist, for the stock. In addition, it helps set a value for buy-out purposes. For future income tax purposes, it helps the surviving partners increase their cost basis in the corporation.

One of the primary disadvantages, especially in this case, is the involvement of so many parties, as we shall see shortly.

2. Entity-purchase. This agreement, also called a stock-redemption plan, is an agreement whereby the corporation itself redeems the shares of the deceased stockholder. In this case, Roger's stock would have been purchased from his wife by the corporation instead of the surviving partners.

One of the advantages of this type of plan is the minimum of paperwork, especially when there are more than two stockholders. There are further advantages if the plan is funded with insurance. On the other hand, there are several disadvantages. First, this type of plan can result in an AMT (alternative minimum tax) problem for the corporation. (However, if it is an S Corporation, there is no AMT problem.) In addition, there is no step-up in the cost basis as with the cross-purchase plan. And finally, the entity-purchase plan may significantly change the ownership status for the remaining shareholders. For example, the person who was a 50-percent stockholder may now end up owning a controlling interest. This was the most popular plan until 1986. Due to changes in the tax laws resulting in the alternative minimum tax, it is no longer as popular as it once was.

3. Wait and see. This is a relatively new type of agreement whereby the parties "wait and see" until there is a death to determine which type of buy-sell agreement (entity-purchase or cross-purchase) to use. As a general rule, at death, the surviving stockholders have the right of first refusal to purchase the stock. If they choose not to do this, it reverts to an entity purchase, and the corporation purchases the stock.

Leaving your business to a family member

If it is your intent to leave your business to a family member, then you might consider making that provision in your will or trust. There is no reason for the heir to pay for something that he or she will inherit anyway. In addition, the business will receive a stepped-up basis for tax purposes. This might create an estate tax problem, however, that you need to consider.

Life insurance in business situations

Throughout this book, I have said that the proper use of life insurance can solve many planning problems. I hate to sound like a broken record, but, again, life insurance comes into play here. All of the problems we have discussed in this chapter have one thing in common: the need for ready, liquid cash. As in many other situations, only life insurance can provide the needed cash at the lowest possible cost.

Let's look at how life insurance fits into the various business situations.

Buy-sell agreements. The use of agreements is great, except for one minor fact: How will the company afford to buy out the deceased stockholder's estate? While many business owners think they can afford to finance this purchase over time, it is not a reasonable solution. Most individuals and companies have enough problems without having to spend precious cash paying off heirs. Why not consider shifting the burden to the insurance company and let it do what it does best? Let's look at each type of agreement.

In the case of a **cross-purchase** agreement, each partner would own and be the beneficiary of a policy on each other. In our example, Roger would have had a policy on each of the other three stockholders, and each of the other three stockholders would have a policy on each other. When Roger died, three policies would have paid benefits to the surviving partners. Each partner would have then purchased Roger's stock from his wife. However, as you can see, this could be cumbersome because there would have had to be 12 separate policies.

With an **entity-purchase**, the corporation would be the owner and beneficiary of a policy on each stockholder. At Roger's death, Midwest Manufacturing would have received the death benefit and purchased his stock from Mrs. Adamson with that money. Only four policies would have been needed—one on each stockholder. But the corporation would have faced AMT ramifications.

In a **wait and see** situation, the insurance would have been structured as if it were a cross-purchase agreement. Therefore, 12 policies would be used. At Roger's death, the surviving shareholders would have had the right of first refusal. If they decided they didn't want to buy the stock, the corporation would have purchased it. To provide the needed cash, each of the surviving shareholders would have loaned the money they received from the insurance on Roger to the corporation. This would have avoided the AMT problems. The corporation would have then purchased the stock.

The primary advantage of using life insurance is that it provides liquidity that is normally absent. Additionally, as we saw in the previous discussion about paying estate taxes, it allows the resolution of a potential problem for a fraction of what the cost might have been.

A new type of insurance that works well in this type of situation is a "first-to-die" policy. This is the opposite of the "second-to-die" policy, which is used for estate taxes. The first-to-die covers several insureds, but only pays the death benefit when the first insured dies. Since only one death benefit has to be paid, the premiums are lower than for two separate policies.

Family business continuation. Life insurance could have played a major part in keeping the Warrens' business out of bankruptcy court. The business faced two problems: bank loans and ownership succession. In the former, the company could have taken out term insurance on Hank's life that would have provided sufficient liquidity to retire the bank debt. This would have relieved Jonathan from worrying about paying off that debt.

Additionally, life insurance could have been used to equalize Hank's estate. Since Ben and Wendy weren't interested in the business, it didn't make sense to leave them stock, let alone make them majority owners. Instead, Hank could have left the stock entirely to Jonathan and taken out life insurance payable to the other children. This would have equalized the estate among the three. If he had done that, the business would still be in operation today. Jonathan would be happy because he would have the business. Ben and Wendy would be happy because they would have an equal amount in cash.

Farm estate taxes. The problem of estate taxes on the farm is not unlike other situations discussed earlier in the book. With proper planning and the use of life insurance, C.B. Franklin would have received sufficient cash at his brother's death to pay the estate taxes. Had he done this, he would be assured of keeping the farm.

Why isn't planning with insurance done more often? A primary reason is the common prejudice against life insurance agents, coupled with a lack of understanding of how to properly use life insurance. Nevertheless, life insurance, properly used, is the only sensible way to solve these tremendous problems to everyone's satisfaction. It is also the cheapest way.

Valuation for estate tax purposes

In the past, it was possible to use a buy-sell agreement to value a closely held business for estate tax purposes. However, recent IRS rulings have changed that. Currently, a buy-sell agreement cannot be depended upon to set the value of the business for closely held businesses. However, there are exceptions. If the agreement meets all of the following, then the valuation set in the agreement can be used for estate tax purposes.

- The agreement must be part of a *bona fide* business arrangement.
- It must not be used to transfer property to family members for less than full consideration.
- The terms must be comparable to similar arrangements entered into by persons in an arm's length transaction.

If all three conditions are met, then the value can be used.

Disability

Don't think that death is the only problem you face with business succession. The disability of one or more of the owners can result in disastrous consequences.

Randy McConnell was a 50-percent owner in a small distribution business. While his partner handled all the business aspects, Randy took care of the warehousing and transportation of the products. One day, while working in the warehouse, he was struck by a forklift and severely injured. He was unable to walk without the aid of a walker, unable to stand for extended periods of time, and obviously unable to lift. As a result, the company had to hire an employee to take his place.

Of course, as with most people in this situation, Randy continued to get paid. But then the company was made aware of a very disturbing fact: because they had no qualified sick pay plan, the wages paid to Randy were not deductible to the business, but they were taxable to him. This was a shock!

This was a bad situation all around. The company was making payments to Randy that it couldn't afford. A replacement had to be hired. It was causing dissension because Randy's partner got sick of making payments for nothing. And all the tax benefits to the company were lost.

Qualified sick pay plan

The easiest way to have solved this problem would have been with a qualified sick pay plan. This is a plan that is established *before* an accident or sickness occurs and contains the following information:

- Who to pay
- How much to pay
- When to start the payments
- How long to pay

As long as this is included, you have a qualified plan, and the payments will be tax-deductible to the company. But that still doesn't resolve the other problem: where is the money going to come from with which to make those payments? The answer is (surprise) insurance.

The proper use of a disability insurance plan, such as discussed previously, will provide the company with the needed funds with which to make those payments. As a result, the company can make the premium payments when everything is going well, and the insurance company will pay when it is needed. There are many IRS regulations that must be met, so this must be handled properly.

Disability buy-out

Besides the buy-sell agreements we covered earlier, you can also have a disability buy-out agreement. This will allow a disabled stockholder to be bought out much the same as would happen at death.

Again, by using insurance to fund this agreement, the financial burden is shifted from the business to the insurance company.

Avoiding taxes on the sale of your business

Although we have discussed disposition upon death, we need to talk about what will happen if you choose to sell your business/practice/farm while you are alive. There are many privately held businesses sold every day for a variety of reasons. In many cases, a sale results in hefty capital gains.

Capital gains taxes can be avoided with the use of a charitable remainder trust discussed in Chapter 19. Review this chapter for details.

This same technique can be used to shelter capital gains on common stock. There are many people who are reluctant to sell a stock because the gain will result in substantial taxes. The CRUT can be used just as effectively in the case of common stock as it was in Jesse Langhorn's case.

Conclusion

Many business owners, farmers and doctors ignore succession and valuation problems. They think that everything will somehow work out satisfactorily. I don't have to tell you that they usually don't. It is a shame to see how many people allow all their hard work to go down the drain for lack of planning.

Twenty-Nine

How Can I Provide for My Disabled Child?

Through the years, we have become more sensitive to the problems faced by disabled children. However, nothing can match the responsibility that the parent of such a child faces.

Unfortunately, unlike so much of our planning, we are dealing with an issue that has no easy solutions. There is no magic wand that can be waived that will solve all your problems. But there are some steps you can take to mentally sort out possible solutions to your concerns.

The needs of a special child

Planning for special children is unusually difficult. In our discussion of minor children, we assumed that a distribution could be made when the child reached a certain age. Such an assumption cannot be made in the case of special children. They have needs that could last beyond your lifetime or your physical ability to handle them. They may outlive their brothers and sisters. Someone has to care for your special children, and that should be part of the planning.

When planning for the special child, some basic questions must be answered concerning care. How are you going to provide for this child for the rest of his or her life? Who is going to be the responsible party?

These are not questions that prompt easy answers. They involve the consideration of various financial assistance programs and the involvement of other family members. However, the biggest mistake is the refusal of parents to face the facts and make the difficult decisions.

It is such a strenuous subject to address that many people just procrastinate until it is too late. This is unfair not only to the child but to the other members of the family. Who better than you is in a position to take action and make the arrangements? Certainly not the probate court.

Governmental assistance programs

The federal government provides several basic programs through Social Security and Medicaid. In addition, you will undoubtedly find some local programs to provide assistance.

Social Security disability benefits. Disability benefits are available to special children if an eligible parent becomes disabled, retires or dies. For the parents to be eligible for Social Security, they must have met the normal Social Security requirements based on work hours. For the child to qualify, he or she must have been disabled prior to age 22 and have been, and still be, unable to work. Social Security's definition of disability is very simple: If you can't work at any job, you are disabled.

Supplemental security income. This program, also through Social Security, is for disabled individuals and is based on need. While under the age of 18, the child must qualify based on the assets and income of his or her parents. Once past that age, he or she qualifies based on his or her own assets and income. The rules are very stringent, and the child is allowed very little in the way of property. As of this writing, the child may have $2,000 in nonexempt property in addition to property specifically exempted, which includes a home, a car and life insurance.

Medicaid. If the special child is eligible for Supplemental Security Income, he or she qualifies for Medicaid. Medicaid is the program that pays for care not covered under Medicare. You may recognize this program from our discussion of long-term care for the aged. Medicaid is the program that pays when the person lacks the resources to do so. You will want to check the current rules for this program in your state.

Government assistance—your decision

In your planning, you must make one basic decision: *Do you or do you not want your child to qualify for governmental assistance?* Lets explore the ramifications of each choice.

Yes, I want my child to qualify for governmental assistance.

If this is your choice, you have three ways to approach it: totally disinherit your child, leave the money to another family member to care for the child or use a trust.

Disinheriting means that upon your death, you leave nothing to the child. Since the child has no funds, he or she qualifies for the programs mentioned previously and becomes a ward of the state. Sometimes, the child will bounce from institution to institution—or get buried in the system. His or her care will be affected by the opening and closing of various government programs. You have no control over your child's welfare and don't know what may happen to him or her.

Leaving the money to another family member means that all your assets belong to that person, not your special child. As a result, you aren't assured that your child will be cared for in the manner you prefer. Any number of things can happen to destroy this plan, such as death of the other party, divorce, financial problems, disagreement; all of those dragons that we have spoken about continually. Remember, that money belongs to the person to whom you leave it, to use as he or she sees fit. There is no guarantee that the child will be any better off than with disinheritance.

A **"special" trust** allows you to leave your instructions for the care of your special child while keeping the assets uncountable for governmental assistance purposes. This trust grants the trustee the power to give what he or she deems appropriate to the child for his care to the point that it will not disqualify him for governmental assistance. For example, the trustee can provide better housing, grant additional spending money or buy items for the child. But the trustee won't duplicate what the government provides. You can include provisions for disposition of the assets of the trust should the child become independent and be able to care for himself.

No, I don't want to qualify my child for assistance.

If this is your desire, then there are several routes to take.

No planning. I hate to list this as an alternative, but it is the course that most people take. They are uncertain as to the proper direction to take and don't feel they can make the tough decisions that we are talking about here. As a result, they do nothing. Obviously, this is the worst thing you can do. All the bad things we talked about earlier in the book come home to roost. Every dragon in the closet finds its way out. The special child ends up inheriting property. But, as with minors, he cannot legally own it. As a result, the child is under the jurisdiction of the probate court. Guardians, who may or may not have a great concern for your child, are appointed. Remember, there are only two reasons for wanting to gain guardianship: love and greed. You've got a living probate process that milks the estate of valuable funds. Nobody knows what action to take. Where should the child live? Where should he go to school? What medical care does he need? What should be his standard of living? It's an unacceptable alternative.

Simple will. Although it is hard to believe, special children are often left money in a simple will. The parents, in a futile attempt to do something, have an attorney draft a will naming a guardian and leaving money to the child. This is only a little better than doing nothing. The only difference is that a guardian is named. All the other problems with leaving property to minor children happen when you leave property to special children, only they are magnified. As with no planning at all, the simple will just isn't a good mechanism for leaving the necessary instructions.

Trust. As in so many cases, a trust will take care of many problems. A trust, either as a part of the will (testamentary) or as a living trust, allows you to leave instructions upon your death. You can name a trustee for your child's funds. You can leave detailed instructions concerning important issues. Assuming you leave sufficient funds, you can care for the needs of your special child for the rest of his or her life. The same issues of a testamentary vs. living trust are encountered here.

Your other children

This is such a touchy issue when special children are involved. Along with all these other difficult decisions, you must resolve how to treat your other children in relation to your special child.

If you decide to disinherit your special child to qualify him for governmental assistance, or if you decide to leave all your money to your other children to care for their sibling, then there are no further decisions to make. You can stop reading at this point.

However, if those choices are not attractive, then we need to look at what else you can do. This time I am going to make the assumption that you agree that some type of trust is necessary, whether it is to qualify your child for governmental assistance or otherwise. Now your decision comes down to this: *Am I going to create one trust for all my children or am I going to create separate trusts?* Let's look at the issues:

One trust. The creation of one trust for all the children puts all your assets in one pot at the death of you and your spouse. Utilizing this trust, your trustee would follow your instructions in handling the finances for the children. You could give the trustee discretion in disbursing the funds, with the emphasis on your special child. At his or her death, the special child's trust would be dissolved and all proceeds distributed. While this has the advantage of allowing you to direct the necessary assets to your special child's needs, it also means that your other children, if the assets are totally consumed by the special child, may never receive their inheritance. Additionally, they must wait until the death of the special child before receiving anything.

Separate trusts. The creation of a separate trust for the special child means you can specify funds for your special child knowing that those dollars cannot be diverted to any of the other children. At the same time, you can either create another trust for your other children or provide for them to receive their inheritance outright. In either case, the money is theirs and cannot be used for your special child. Upon the death of the special child, his funds can be distributed to his brothers and sisters. While this sounds good in theory, it is difficult to know how much to put in the special child's trust—with the concern being that he may run out of funds before he dies.

Which type of trust to use

Decisions, decisions, decisions. It seems this chapter will never end and the choices will go on forever. But, fear not. We are getting close to the end. By now we have narrowed the decision-making process, and hopefully we have triggered your thinking in the appropriate direction. Assuming you feel the trust is the only route to take, another choice must be made: *Will the trust be a revocable living trust, an irrevocable living trust, or a testamentary trust?*

The **irrevocable living trust** involves setting up a trust and transferring property into it. However, the transfer of property to an irrevocable living trust constitutes a gift and must be considered in that light. Once you establish the trust, the terms cannot be changed, so while it does have the advantage of possibly reducing estate taxes in the future by "freezing" the value of the gift, the property cannot be reclaimed.

A **revocable living trust** involves setting up a trust and titling your property into it. As discussed previously, the revocable trust is totally under your control (assuming you are the trustee) and can be canceled or changed anytime you wish.

A **testamentary trust** is established at your death as a result of your will. While your will (and thus your trust) can be changed during your life, it becomes irrevocable upon your death. It carries with it the advantages and disadvantages discussed earlier.

Funding the trust

One final decision must be made: *How are you going to fund the trust in order to be fair to all your children?*

Fairness is a really thorny issue when it comes to families with special children. In these families, not much is fair. The other children usually feel they are getting the short end of the stick as more attention and funds are directed to the special child. This is not right or wrong; this is reality. Fortunately in most households, the other children understand and support the position of the parents. Nevertheless, you still have the problem of how to distribute your assets to your children, and that comes down to a function of money.

Repeating what was said at the beginning of the chapter, there are no good solutions to this problem. It is just that some are better than others. If you set up separate trusts, then the special child may run out of money. If you set up one trust for all the children, the other children may never receive their inheritance.

If you don't have sufficient assets to care for the special child while allowing the other children to receive the inheritance you desire, then the most equitable solution to the dilemma is the use of life insurance. Separate trusts can be set up with life insurance used to fund either the special child's trust or the trust of your other children, or both. If you are especially concerned with the special child but have sufficient assets, you can leave your assets to him or her and fund the other children's trust with life insurance. If you can possibly estimate a dollar amount the special child might need, you can fund that trust with life insurance and leave the remainder of your property to the others. And with the irrevocable life insurance trust we discussed earlier, these dollars can pass outside your estate.

Conclusion

The fact is that planning can be accomplished to take care of *all* your children, but it must be done carefully and with compassion. The worst thing you can do is ignore the problem and hope it goes away. The best thing you can do is take care of the problems *in advance* by doing some planning that takes into consideration the needs of each and every one of your children.

Thirty

How Can I Protect My Family in a Second Marriage?

A generation ago, it was rare to see second marriages. Now, second, third and fourth are common. And with these additional families come additional problems, especially in the estate planning field.

Let's look at the typical scenario in a second marriage:

Bill and Nancy Glenn had been married five years, and both had children from a previous marriage. They had their attorney draw up a will. As is typical, Bill's will left everything to Nancy, if living, otherwise to his children. Nancy's will left everything to Bill, if living, otherwise to her children. This scenario is carried out every day of the year in different towns across America.

Bill died in a tragic accident. Nancy received his property according to his will (and the balance of the property by virtue of her being the surviving joint tenant and beneficiary). As time goes by, Nancy may remarry. In that case, what about Bill's children? They're living with their mother. Nancy doesn't have much to do with them anymore. But she has all their dad's property.

Most likely, they will end up with nothing. And vice versa. If she dies first, Bill ends up with it all, and his will leaves everything to his kids. Her kids are out in the cold.

This is a problem that very few people recognize, and it brings up the Rosenberg Law of Second Marriages: The children of the first to die lose! Not a very comforting thought.

Concerns in a second marriage

But how else can it be handled? Let's look at Bill's concerns.

- He loves Nancy, and wants to make sure that she is taken care of if he dies first, so he can't leave everything outright to his children.
- Since Bill has minor children and their natural mother has custody, he doesn't want to leave money to the children, otherwise his ex-wife will have control of it.
- If the children are in college when he dies, he wants to make sure they have money for their education, but he doesn't want all the money to go to them in a lump sum.

Use of a trust

What's the solution? By now you should know: a trust. Either a testamentary trust as part of the will, or a living trust. The trust will specify that certain property will go into a Q-TIP trust for Nancy's benefit. She can have the interest off the property, and if she needs money for emergencies, the trustee can give it to her. But upon her death, the property goes to Bill's children. The same is done in Nancy's trust.

Bill can also leave separate funds in a trust for the children and name a trustee. If he has confidence in his ex-wife, he can name her as trustee for the children. He can indicate how and when the children should receive their property.

In other words, with some planning, everyone can be taken care of. The beauty of using a trust is that it can be structured to meet all their goals. If they have "his, hers, and ours" children, the trust can provide for the care of all of them.

Ray, age 67, is married to Leslie, age 40. Ray has three children, ranging in ages from 25 to 41. He has some very real planning goals: He wants to take care of Leslie; he doesn't want his children to have to wait until Leslie dies before they receive any inheritance; and he feels that the longer he is married, the more he will want to leave Leslie. Ray entered the marriage with about $1.5 million in property, Leslie with $5,000. Additionally, Ray's younger son is somewhat irresponsible, so Ray doesn't want him to receive his share all at once.

It was determined that a living trust would be best for several reasons. Ray's and Leslie's estate would avoid both living and death probate. Ray could be initial trustee and could name successor trustees, which would include one of Ray's children, to take care of him if he became disabled. The trust would help them reduce their estate taxes. The trust could establish sub-trusts to take care of Leslie; and they could easily change the terms as the marriage matured. This would also serve to equalize the estate, since previously, if Leslie died first, she wouldn't have had $600,000 to put into the family Trust. If they used a testamentary trust instead of a living trust, Ray would have to title property in Leslie's name alone, which he is uncomfortable doing at this point in their marriage.

At Ray's death, $600,000 will go into a family trust for his children. The two older children will get their money immediately. The youngest will receive his over a period of time. Two other sub-trusts will be established for Leslie. The marital trust will consist of a certain amount of money, with the balance going into the Q-TIP Trust. She will have full access to the marital trust, which will include the home. She will receive income from the Q-TIP with principal as needed for health. Leslie, along with Ray's daughter (with whom she has good rapport), will be co-trustees of that trust. After Leslie's death, Ray's children will get the balance of the property.

Leslie's instructions in the trust are different, since Ray wants access to the money if she dies first. She realizes that all the assets coming into the marriage are from Ray, and she isn't greedy. She is happy that he cares enough to take care of her so well after such a short period of time. And, knowing Ray as I do, he will make the terms more liberal as the years pass.

This is just one example, but it shows how proper planning can accomplish your goals, no matter how complicated they may seem. Some situations take a lot more planning and thinking than others, but those are the most fun to work on. What may seem overwhelming to you is merely an exciting challenge to a professional.

To Borrow a Phrase, "Just Do It!"

As you know by now, proper planning is vital to your financial security and that of your loved ones. You are now familiar with enough concepts to start taking necessary action. That process begins by reviewing your situation, determining your goals, choosing the proper techniques, and meeting with the necessary legal and financial advisors.

Let's take one last look at our definition.

"During my life and after my death, I want to control and distribute my property in the manner I desire, minimizing all fees, taxes and court interference, preserving for myself, my family, and those I choose, the estate I have worked so hard to create."

As stated previously, this is not a do-it-yourself book. With all the tools and techniques available, improper execution can cause disastrous results. Hopefully, you will use this opportunity to seek out *professionals* who can help you effect meaningful planning. But that may be easier said than done.

If I can be of service, don't hesitate to contact me. I regularly speak before groups and companies on matters dealing with financial and estate planning, in addition to consulting with individuals and businesses. For information, call (800) 777-0867 or write to me at 2517 Moody Road, Warner Robins, GA 31088.

About the Author

Stephen M. Rosenberg, CFP, is president of Rosenberg Asset Management, where he specializes in estate and financial planning. Besides being a recognized authority on matters dealing with estate planning, he teaches graduate level finance courses for a major university. He is co-author of *Every Woman's Guide To Financial Security* and has appeared on radio and television from coast to coast, including CNN, CNBC, and ABC, NBC, and CBS affiliates. In addition, he has been quoted and interviewed for national magazines and newspapers. He works with clients and speaks to organizations and groups on a variety of financial topics. Mr. Rosenberg can be reached at (800) 777-0867 or (912) 922-8100.

Index

Index